Eyewitness
VIETNAM WAR

VC guerrillas
demonstrate ambush

Vietminh medal
for bravery

Soviet-made 7D
grenade launcher

US lensatic
military compass

US military
dog tags

Peace-symbol
badge

Montagnard
crossbow and
arrows

PENICILLIN

Chinese-made
penicillin, used by
the Viet Cong

MADDOX

731

USS Maddox uniform patch

Eyewitness
VIETNAM WAR

Written by
STUART MURRAY

DK

Lyndon B.
Johnson 1964
campaign button

North Vietnamese Air
Force symbol

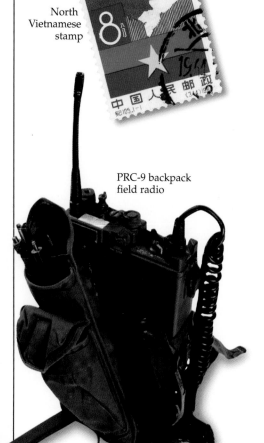

North
Vietnamese
stamp

PRC-9 backpack
field radio

M-1 bayonet

LONDON, NEW YORK, MELBOURNE,
MUNICH, and DELHI

DK Publishing, Inc.
Senior Editor Barbara Berger
Senior Designer Tai Blanche
Additional Design Jeremy Canceko,
Jee Chang, and Jessica Lasher
Assistant Managing Art Editor Michelle Baxter
Creative Director Tina Vaughan
Jacket Art Director Dirk Kaufman
Production Manager Ivor Parker
DTP Coordinator Milos Orlovic

Media Projects, Inc.
Executive Editor Carter Smith
Project Editor Aaron R. Murray
Associate Editor Margaret C.F. McLaughlin
Production Manager James A. Burmester
Consultants Clifford J. Rogers and Steve R. Waddell,
United States Military Academy
Cartography Ron Toelke, Rob Stokes
Picture Researcher Erika Rubel
Copy Editor Glenn Novak

First published in Great Britain in 2005
by Dorling Kindersley Limited,
80 Strand, London WC2R 0RL

05 06 07 08 09 10 9 8 7 6 5 4 3 2 1

Published in the United States by DK Publishing, Inc.

A CIP catalogue for this book is
available from the British Library.

ISBN 1 4053 1133 9

Colour reproduction by Colourscan, Singapore
Printed in China by Toppan Printing Co.,(Shenzhen) Ltd.

Discover more at
www.dk.com

US infantry helmet

South Vietnamese
200-dong note, 1966

Soviet-made antitank
land mine

Chinese cobra

Contents

US M-16A1
assault rifle

War in French Indochina

INDOCHINA STAMP
France issued postage stamps for its colonies in Indochina, such as this stamp from 1907.

THE GLOBAL DESTRUCTION caused by World War II (1939–1945) weakened France's colonial empire. During the war, the Japanese took control of French colonies in the Indochina Peninsula of Southeast Asia. In 1945, Vietnamese nationalists took up arms to gain independence. Led by Ho Chi Minh (1890–1969), a Communist, they first battled the occupying Japanese forces.

Many fighters in Ho's nationalist army, known as the Vietminh, were trained by advisors from the United States, which was at war with Japan. After Japan's defeat, France wanted to re-establish control over Indochina, but Ho declared Vietnam's independence. He tried to negotiate with the French, but they would not recognize Vietnam. The stage was set for the First Indochina War.

EMPEROR BAO DAI
European-educated Bao Dai (1913–1997), shown above with French officials in the 1920s, was the 13th and last emperor of Vietnam. He was recognized by France as the country's ruler, but to Vietnamese nationalists he was a French puppet – they wanted an independent republic with elected rulers.

Vietnamese dragon

Bao Dai stamp

Japanese "Rising Sun" battle flag

JAPANESE WARSHIPS
Japan's battleships patrol Indochinese waters as her troops on land fight the Communist-led Vietminh nationalists. Ho Chi Minh's army gained valuable military experience fighting against the Japanese.

US ADVISORS TRAIN VIETMINH
An American military advisor looks on as Vietminh fighters practise throwing grenades. The Vietminh included Communist and non-Communist nationalists. After the war, Ho Chi Minh won support from Communist countries – the People's Republic of China and the Soviet Union. The United States objected to Communist influence over the growing independence movements of French Indochina.

Map of Vietnam

Portrait of Ho Chi Minh

Early currency of the Democratic Republic of Vietnam (DRV)

DECLARING INDEPENDENCE
Ho Chi Minh, right, addresses Vietnamese nationalists gathered in the northern Vietnamese city of Hanoi, below, on 2 September 1945, the day of Japan's surrender. Ho declared the establishment of the independent Democratic Republic of Vietnam (DRV). At first, the French granted limited freedoms to the DRV, but clashes followed between Vietnamese government forces and French troops. As growing hostility between the DRV and France made war unavoidable, the United States backed French domination of Vietnam.

FRENCH MILITARY PARADE
Newly arrived French soldiers drive through Hanoi past cheering French colonial residents and their Vietnamese supporters. The French tried to re-establish military control in Indochina just after World War II. Some Vietnamese favoured French rule and bitterly opposed the Vietminh nationalists – especially as the Vietminh became increasingly influenced by Communism. Many of the French-allied Vietnamese were educated in Europe, and had converted from Buddhism to Catholicism.

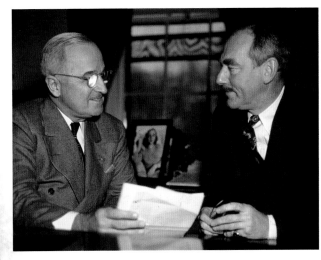

TRUMAN AND ACHESON
US president Harry S. Truman (1884–1972), left, meets with Secretary of State Dean Acheson (1893–1971) in the late 1940s. Both believed that if Vietnam were controlled by Ho's Communists, then other Indochinese countries also would become Communist. Acheson persuaded Truman to give France financial and military aid to oppose the Communists and the DRV.

INDOCHINA TIMELINE

1940 Japan takes over French Indochina in World War II.

1941 Ho Chi Minh establishes the Vietminh, the "League for the Independence of Vietnam".

1945 Japan surrenders. Ho Chi Minh forms the Democratic Republic of Vietnam (DRV).

1946 French colonial troops clash with DRV forces, sparking the First Indochina War (1946–1954).

1950 French suffer defeats; United States sets up the Military Assistance and Advisory Group (MAAG) to further aid France.

1951 France controls cities; Vietminh control countryside.

1954 Vietminh take Dien Pien Phu base and defeat French, ending First Indochina War. Treaty in Geneva, Switzerland, temporarily divides Vietnam into North and South, calls for vote on Vietnamese future.

France loses Indochina

Eᴀʀʟʏ ɪɴ ᴛʜᴇ Fɪʀsᴛ Iɴᴅᴏᴄʜɪɴᴀ Wᴀʀ, American military supplies and equipment gave the French an advantage over the Vietminh. The French captured the cities, but Ho Chi Minh and his top general, Vo Nguyen Giap (b. 1912), were unwilling to accept defeat. They reorganized their army in the jungles and mountains and received aid from Communist China. The war went on for years. In late 1953, the French built a new base at Dien Bien Phu, in the northern mountains. By the spring, Colonel Christian de Castries and 15,000 troops were surrounded there by Giap's 55,000 men and hundreds of artillery pieces. After a 55-day siege, De Castries surrendered in May 1954. The victorious Vietminh prepared for an independent Vietnam.

Canteen

ASSAULT FROM THE AIR
French paratroopers land at Dien Bien Phu in late 1953 to establish a new base. By next spring, Vietminh artillery had destroyed the French airfield, and ground attacks were capturing French positions one by one. The whole world watched the battle raging at Dien Bien Phu.

FACING IMPOSSIBLE ODDS
In a bunker at Dien Bien Phu, Colonel De Castries (1902–1991) faces surrender or death. His force was completely cut off from help and under heavy bombardment by Vietminh artillery. De Castries was taken prisoner, but survived captivity and returned home.

Sandbags protect walls

US military gear used by French

PLANNING A FRENCH DEFEAT
Vietminh leader Ho Chi Minh, left, studies the layout of besieged Dien Bien Phu, a French base in the mountains on the Vietnam–Laos border. Along with Ho is General Vo Nguyen Giap, right, who commanded Vietminh forces in the battle. Although the French won several major clashes during the war, in the end Giap and Ho outgeneralled them.

Soldier's bundled bedding and coat

DOOMED FRENCH DEFENDERS
After fighting bravely for almost two months, these weary French troops wait for the end to come. They had not expected the Vietminh to drag cannon into the mountains and bombard their base. Approximately 2,000 French troops and 8,000 Vietminh died in the campaign, with 10,800 French captured. Most of the captives died of hunger and disease.

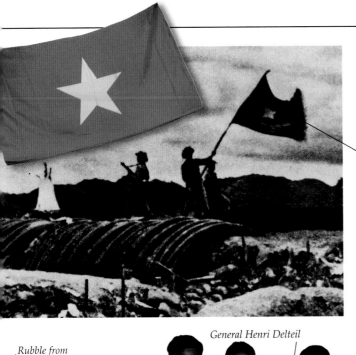

FRENCH HEADQUARTERS BUNKER FALLS
Victorious Vietnamese fighters raise their red and gold flag over Colonel De Castries's steel-covered bunker. This central command centre fell to the Vietminh on 7 May 1954, after a siege of 55 days. One soldier waves the flag while two others stand guard. Seven weeks later, a veteran French armoured battalion, Groupement Mobile (GM) 100, was ambushed on the road and almost completely destroyed by the Vietminh. This decisive defeat, combined with the fall of Dien Bien Phu, ended the First Indochina War.

Communist flag

The Geneva Accords

Peace terms ending the First Indochina War were signed in Geneva, Switzerland, by the French and the Vietminh, on 20 July 1954. Known as the Geneva Accords, they gave the Communists control of Vietnam north of the 17th parallel. A non-Communist government ruled South Vietnam. The Vietnamese were to hold elections within two years to decide on their form of government. The United States opposed a Communist-led Vietnam, however, and refused to accept the accords or an election.

Rubble from artillery bombardment

General Henri Delteil

North Vietnam

17th parallel

South Vietnam

Value of stamp

Communist star

英勇的越南南方
人民必胜
国际工会支援越南南方
工人和人民委员会

8

中国人民邮政

INDOCHINA TRUCE SIGNING
Former French general Henri Delteil signs truce documents on 20 July 1954, ending Indochina hostilities. A European official and Vietnamese delegates look on during the ceremony in Geneva's Palace of Nations. Month-long negotiations were held in the palace before the signing.

DIVIDED VIETNAM
This North Vietnamese stamp shows Vietnam separated into North and South by a line at the 17th parallel. The South China Sea is blue, at right, and Communist China is north. The former French colonies of Laos and Cambodia are to the left. They became independent in the mid-1950s.

Vietminh medal for bravery

VICTORY PARADE
Triumphant Vietminh troops driving military trucks through Hanoi in October 1954 are cheered on by crowds lining the city streets. French colonial forces had recently pulled out of Hanoi and departed for South Vietnam. After almost eight years of war this northern city was now under the complete control of Vietminh forces. Hanoi became North Vietnam's capital.

Dien Bien Phu to Armistice

- **1953** 90,000 French troops in Vietnam, with 100,000 Vietnamese National Army (colonial) troops; Vietminh forces number 200,000.
- **November 1953** French build base at Dien Bien Phu.
- **December 1953** French troops assemble at Dien Bien Phu, prepare for major battle.
- **February 1954** Giap surrounds Dien Bien Phu.
- **13 March 1954** Vietminh start ground assaults.
- **1 May 1954** Final ground attacks begin.
- **7 May 1954** Dien Bien Phu falls.
- **24 June–17 July 1954** GM 100, a 3,000-strong armoured unit, wiped out.
- **1 August 1954** Armistice ends the First Indochina War.

US advisors in Vietnam

THE "Advisory Phase" began in 1955, as President Dwight D. Eisenhower (1890–1969) sent hundreds of military advisors to aid the Republic of (South) Vietnam (RVN). The Eisenhower administration wanted to prevent the spread of Communism in Southeast Asia. It helped anti-Communist Ngo Dinh Diem (1901–1963) take power in a corrupt election that year. Thousands of angry South Vietnamese armed to fight Diem's government. Diem called them "Viet Cong" (VC), meaning Vietnamese Communists. These anti-Diem forces were led by the National Liberation Front (NLF), an alliance of political groups. The NLF was headquartered in the North, while VC guerrillas fought in the South. When John F. Kennedy (1917–1963) became US president in 1961, he increased American involvement. In late 1963, Diem was overthrown and killed, and Kennedy was assassinated.

IN FLIGHT
Refugees from northern Vietnam rush southward in 1954 to escape Hanoi's new Communist government. Other Vietnamese, favouring communism, chose to move north.

IN JUNGLE WATERS
US military advisors and troops from the Army of the Republic of Vietnam (ARVN) keep gear dry as they cross a muddy river in 1963. More than 14,000 US military advisors were serving in Vietnam by then.

Grenade launcher

US Army-issue helmet

FIRST PRESIDENT OF SOUTH VIETNAM
Diem speaks at his 1955 inauguration. He removed Emperor Bao Dai as head of state and punished political opponents. A Roman Catholic, Diem favoured members of his own religion even though the nation was 80 percent Buddhist.

200
Và
314667
NGÂN HÀNG QUỐC GIA VIỆT NAM
HAI TRAM ĐỒNG
314667

South Vietnamese 200-dong note, 1966

19th-century Vietnamese hero Nguyen Hué

AN ANGRY PROTEST
Buddhists struggle with police in Saigon during a demonstration against Diem's government in 1963. The protesters objected to persecution of their faith and called for peaceful negotiations with the Communists. Diem also was opposed by ARVN and US military leaders, who felt he was ineffective in destroying the VC.

Sacks of personal possessions

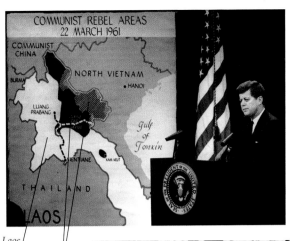

COMMUNIST REBEL AREAS 22 MARCH 1961

COMMUNIST CHINA

NORTH VIETNAM

• HANOI

BURMA

LUANG PRABANG

Gulf of Tonkin

KAK NEUT

VIENTIANE

THAILAND

LAOS

Laos

Communist-controlled regions of Laos are shaded

JFK'S WAR
President Kennedy gives a press conference on the threat of Communist power in Southeast Asia in 1961. During his presidency, more than $500 million in US military aid flowed each year to South Vietnam. JFK's administration disliked Diem's corrupt government. The United States did not publicly object when ARVN generals executed Diem on 1 November 1963.

REVIEWING A BATTLE PLAN
Colonel John Paul Vann (1924–1972), left, examines a map with ARVN and US officers. Vann was a key figure in MAAG – the US Military Assistance and Advisory Group, which oversaw the advisors in Vietnam. He objected to the careless use of heavy firepower. He preferred winning the loyalty of the people, and publicly spoke out for more effective South Vietnamese leadership.

MAAG uniform patch

CONSPIRATORS AGAINST DIEM
Ambitious ARVN generals led by Duong Van Minh, near right, murdered President Diem in November 1963 and took over the government. These men were soon overthrown by other generals eager to rule South Vietnam. As US involvement escalated the republic was rocked by military coups (overthrows).

KENNEDY'S ASSASSINATION
President Kennedy and First Lady Jacqueline Kennedy were riding in a motorcade through Dallas on 22 November 1963, when he was shot by a sniper. Vice President Lyndon B. Johnson, below, took the oath of office with Mrs Kennedy at his side. Historians disagree over whether JFK would have escalated US involvement in Vietnam – which LBJ did.

CHICAGO DAILY NEWS

PRESIDENT IS KILLED

Texas Sniper Escapes; Johnson Sworn In

JFK's limousine

Story Begins on Next Page

Chicago Daily News front page coverage of JFK's assasination

THE MAIN PLAYERS

- **ARVN** Army of the Republic of (South) Vietnam; rose from Vietnamese National Army (former French allies).
- **RVN** Republic of (South) Vietnam.
- **DRV** Democratic Republic of (North) Vietnam.
- **NLF** National Liberation Front, organized by Ho in 1960.
- **MAAG** Military Assistance and Advisory Group, formed by US in 1950 to aid France in Indochina. Replaced by **MACV** (Military Assistance Command, Vietnam) in 1962.

Gulf of Tonkin Incident

IN THE SUMMER OF 1964, the US destroyer *Maddox* was operating in the Gulf of Tonkin, close to North Vietnam, conducting electronic surveillance (gathering information) for secret ARVN and US raids on North Vietnamese naval bases. On 2 August, the *Maddox* was fired on by torpedo boats challenging her presence in North Vietnamese waters. The *Maddox* returned fire and called in air support. One torpedo boat was sunk; the others escaped. *Maddox* commander Herbert L. Ogier's report went directly to President Johnson. Two nights later, Ogier's electronics operators thought another attack was developing. The ship fired into the darkness and manoeuvred against torpedoes that seemed to be heading its way. LBJ now ordered airstrikes on North Vietnamese coastal installations. On 7 August, Congress passed the Gulf of Tonkin Resolution, giving him broad war powers. Although it became clear the *Maddox* crew had been mistaken about the second attack, LBJ's course was set. He committed the United States to waging war against Vietnamese Communists.

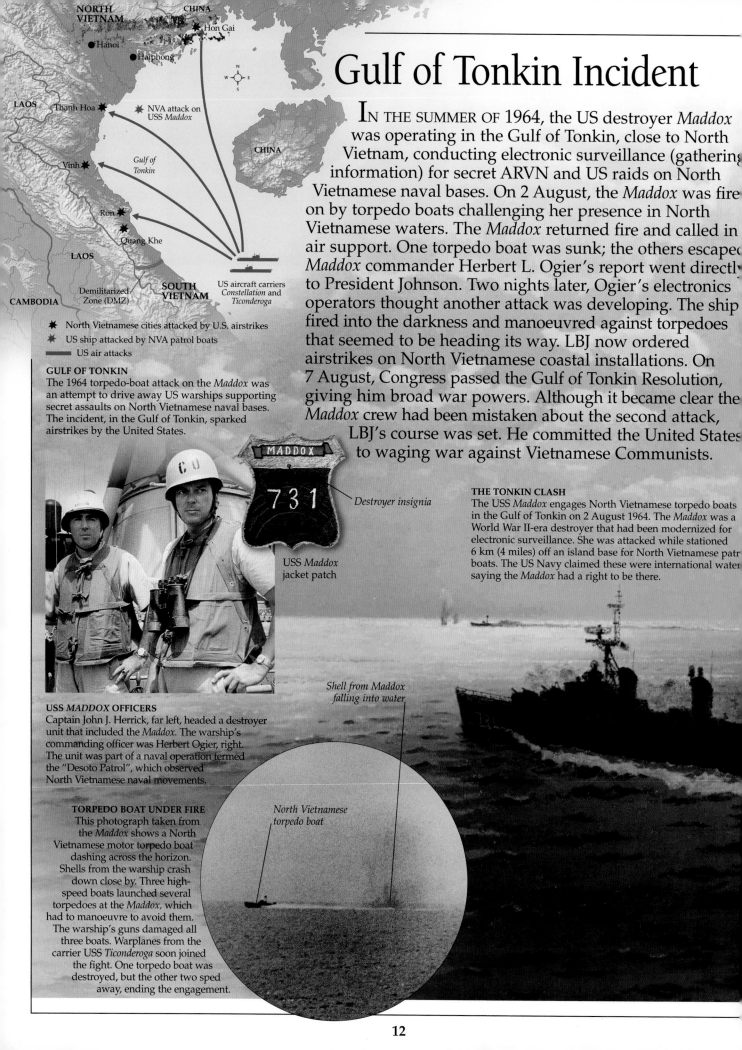

NVA attack on USS Maddox

Gulf of Tonkin

US aircraft carriers Constellation and Ticonderoga

✷ North Vietnamese cities attacked by U.S. airstrikes
✷ US ship attacked by NVA patrol boats
— US air attacks

GULF OF TONKIN
The 1964 torpedo-boat attack on the *Maddox* was an attempt to drive away US warships supporting secret assaults on North Vietnamese naval bases. The incident, in the Gulf of Tonkin, sparked airstrikes by the United States.

Destroyer insignia

USS Maddox jacket patch

THE TONKIN CLASH
The USS *Maddox* engages North Vietnamese torpedo boats in the Gulf of Tonkin on 2 August 1964. The *Maddox* was a World War II-era destroyer that had been modernized for electronic surveillance. She was attacked while stationed 6 km (4 miles) off an island base for North Vietnamese patrol boats. The US Navy claimed these were international waters, saying the *Maddox* had a right to be there.

USS MADDOX OFFICERS
Captain John J. Herrick, far left, headed a destroyer unit that included the *Maddox*. The warship's commanding officer was Herbert Ogier, right. The unit was part of a naval operation termed the "Desoto Patrol", which observed North Vietnamese naval movements.

Shell from Maddox falling into water

TORPEDO BOAT UNDER FIRE
This photograph taken from the *Maddox* shows a North Vietnamese motor torpedo boat dashing across the horizon. Shells from the warship crash down close by. Three high-speed boats launched several torpedoes at the *Maddox*, which had to manoeuvre to avoid them. The warship's guns damaged all three boats. Warplanes from the carrier USS *Ticonderoga* soon joined the fight. One torpedo boat was destroyed, but the other two sped away, ending the engagement.

North Vietnamese torpedo boat

US F-8 Crusader jet

AIR CAMPAIGN BEGINS
A US warplane roars from the deck of the aircraft carrier USS *Constellation* in August 1964. Bombers struck North Vietnamese naval bases in the Gulf of Tonkin. In spring 1965, the air attacks expanded into Operation Rolling Thunder, the bombing of North Vietnam's supply routes and munitions storage areas (see pages 20–21). This three-year campaign was interrupted several times as LBJ attempted unsuccessfully to make the Communists negotiate.

The deck of a carrier was twice the size of a football pitch

McNAMARA DEFENDS WAR
US defence secretary Robert S. McNamara (b. 1916) points to a map showing the Gulf of Tonkin. McNamara is explaining the *Maddox* clash to the Washington press corps on 4 August 1964. The attack was termed the "Gulf of Tonkin Incident". McNamara announced the United States was now "moving substantial military reinforcements" to Southeast Asia.

NAVY AND MARINE CORPS MEDAL
This medal is awarded to Navy personnel for heroism in noncombat situations. Naval duties are often dangerous, especially at sea, and can require outstanding acts of courage.

North Vietnamese torpedo boat

Maddox's cannon fires on torpedo boats

US M-14 rifle

"Americanization" of the conflict

Although there was no formal declaration of war, President Johnson fully used the war powers of the Gulf of Tonkin Resolution. He committed the US military to Vietnam in a policy known as the "Americanization" of the war. He hoped US military strength would persuade the Communists to accept the South Vietnamese government. In addition to the Rolling Thunder air campaign, LBJ now sent troops to South Vietnam to protect US military installations. The first Marines arrived by landing craft on beaches near Da Nang in March 1965. Soldiers soon were in action against the Viet Cong. This first large-scale American military involvement marked the end of the advisory period in Vietnam.

The Americanization phase of the Second Indochina War – better known as the Vietnam War – had begun. By July 1965 more than 50,000 US troops were in South Vietnam.

MARINES HIT THE BEACH
Marines splash ashore near Da Nang, South Vietnam, on 18 March 1965. They are heading for an airfield they have been assigned to protect against VC attacks. Additional US forces were arriving at other places, and American television showed many of these events. This was the first military conflict to be seen on television.

Communist and US allies

ALLIES WERE IMPORTANT TO THE US and South Vietnamese war effort, but they were even more crucial to the Communists. The United States and South Vietnam could have waged war without Allied support, but the Vietnamese Communists did not have the industrial might to arm the troops they needed. North Vietnam and the Viet Cong received military supplies and financial aid from Communist China and the Soviet Union. American and RVN forces were supported by the "Free World Forces": troops from South Korea and nations in the Southeast Asia Treaty Organization (SEATO). South Korea sent the most troops to Vietnam – 312,000. Australia was next, with 47,000. The Philippines, Thailand, and New Zealand also contributed troops to fight against the Communists.

ALLIED PROPAGANDA
In this South Vietnamese poster, Allied nations are represented by flags on the top left. They offer bags of grain and a bowl of rice to help the Vietnamese, while the Soviet Union, on the right, offers only guns and destruction.

CHINESE MUNITIONS
This Chinese-made 120-mm mortar round was captured at a VC supply base in Cambodia, before it could be transported to guerrillas fighting in South Vietnam.

DRV prime minister Pham Van Dong (1906–2000)

DRV (Nor Vietnames flag

Clasped hands

FRIENDS' DECORATION
The Vietnamese inscription on this medal, awarded to foreigners who aided the DRV, reads "Solidarity against American aggression".

SOVIET MONEY
The USSR provided financial aid to Vietnamese Communists. Shown here is a Soviet 10-ruble note.

Portrait of Soviet premier Vladimir Ilich Lenin

A WARM WELCOME TO CHINA
North Vietnamese Communist Party heads and government officials receive an enthusiastic greeting from the Chinese premier, Zhou En-lai, on a state visit to Beijing, the Chinese capital, in 1973.

Vietnamese Communist Party leader Le Duan (1908–1986)

Chinese premier Zhou En-lai (1898–1976)

Cuban Communist Party leader Blas Roca (1908–1987)

North Vietnamese president Ho Chi Minh (1890–1969)

Soviet premier Nikita Khrushchev (1894–1971)

Hungarian Party leader Janos Kadar (1912–1989)

Soviet president Leonid Brezhnev (1906–1982)

HO IN RUSSIA
Ho Chi Minh, second from left, joins Soviet officials and leaders from other Communist states to view a military parade in Moscow in 1961. The Soviet are celebrating the Russian Revolution that brought Communis to power in 1917.

RVN prime minister Nguyen Cao Ky (b. 1930)

Australian prime minister Harold Holt (1908–1967)

South Korean president Park Chung Hee (1917–1979)

Philippines president Ferdinand Marcos (1917–1989)

New Zealand prime minister Keith Holyoake (1904–1983)

RVN chief of state Nguyen Van Thieu (1923–2001)

Thai prime minister Thanom Kittikachorn (1912–2004)

US president Lyndon Johnson (1908–1973)

SEATO LEADERS CONFER IN MANILA

Heads of the SEATO nations and nonmembers South Korea and South Vietnam meet in the Philippine capital, Manila, to discuss the Indochina conflict, in October 1966. SEATO was founded in September 1954 under the direction of the United States. Its purpose was to prevent more Southeast Asian countries from falling under Communist rule. SEATO's main task was to support the US military presence in Vietnam. SEATO was disbanded in 1977.

FREE WORLD FORCES HANG TAG
This ID tag was attached to a button and worn on the shirts of troops who were termed by the Allies as "Free World Forces."

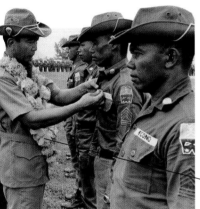

PHILIPPINE AWARDS
President Marcos pins medals on Filipino soldiers being honoured in Vietnam for bravery and outstanding achievements, in July 1967. He was visiting their headquarters in Tay Ninh, South Vietnam. The first Filipino troops arrived in Indochina in the summer of 1966.

Flower wreath given to welcome President Marcos

Australian service medal

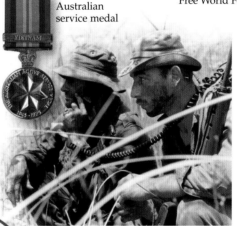

AUSSIE AMBUSH
Members of the 7th Australian Royal Regiment communicate by radio while setting up an ambush in Vietnamese hill country. "Aussies" usually operated guerrilla-style. In 1966, a 101-man combat team fought off an assault by more than 2,500 VC at Long Tan.

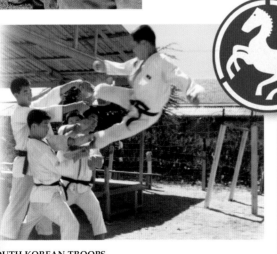

South Korean White Horse division patch

US-made M-1 carbine

SOUTH KOREAN TROOPS
Above, a Korean martial arts instructor demonstrates a flying kick, in 1968. At right, Koreans stand guard over VC guerrillas just taken prisoner, c1966. South Koreans composed the third-largest Allied army, after the United States and South Vietnam. Koreans were among the most aggressive of the Free World Forces. They maintained three full divisions in Vietnam: White Horse, Blue Dragon, and Tiger.

The leaders

A⟙ THE START OF THE VIETNAM WAR, Vietnamese Communist leaders had been in power for more than 20 years. They had vast experience in military organization and guerrilla tactics. American and South Vietnamese leaders, on the other hand, were mostly politicians with little military experience. Ho Chi Minh and Vo Nguyen Giap stayed in power for most of the war, while US and RVN leaders came and went. The Communists fought with all their might, but the United States had to conduct a "limited war". This meant trying to use only enough force to make the Communists stop fighting. The United States did not want to employ its great military power to destroy North Vietnam.

HO CHI MINH (1890–1969)
"Uncle Ho", as his people called him, symbolized Vietnamese patriotism. Ho's struggle against French and Japanese occupation prepared him for the Vietnam War. He died before the final Communist triumph in 1975.

NGUYEN HUU THO (1910–1996)
Tho was a French-educated lawyer who became chairman of the National Liberation Front. Imprisoned by the Ngo Dinh Diem regime, Tho escaped, and went on to lead Viet Cong guerrilla forces. After the war, Tho became vice president of Vietnam.

VO NGUYEN GIAP (b. 1912)
General Giap led Communist forces in Vietnam from the 1940s to 1972. His military career was a great success, but younger generals took over for the last years of the war. Giap retired as minister of national defence in 1980.

"We are determined to fight for independence, national unity, democracy, and peace."

HO CHI MINH IN A PROCLAMATIO[N] ON 8 MAY 1954

TRAN DO (1923–2002)
Tran Do was deputy commander of Viet Cong forces operating in South Vietnam. Do, who fought against the French, was also a general in the North Vietnamese army and a high-ranking member of the Communist Party. Years after the war, he fell out of favour with the Communist-led national government for criticizing the slow development of Vietnamese democracy.

PHAM VAN DONG (1908–2000)
In 1930, Dong helped Ho Chi Minh found the Indo-chinese Communist Party. He became prime minister of North Vietnam in 1950. Dong, right, walks with Cambodia's Prince Norodom Sihanouk.

NGUYEN VAN THIEU (1924–2001)
Shown voting in an election, Thieu was president of South Vietnam from 1967 to 1973. During the First Indochina War, he fought for the Vietminh army but then changed sides. He joined French colonial forces and later rose to power in South Vietnam. Thieu often attempted to control ARVN units in the field. This angered his generals, who had their own plans.

WILLIAM C. WESTMORELAND (b. 1914)
A veteran leader, General Westmoreland was commander of US forces in Vietnam when the first American combat troops landed in 1965. He led US forces in Vietnam until he was replaced by Creighton Abrams in 1968.

NGUYEN CAO KY (b. 1930)
A South Vietnamese fighter pilot and air force leader, General Ky was the premier in President Thieu's government from 1965 to 1971. Ky was often in the news, seen wearing flashy uniforms. When Saigon fell to the Communists in 1975, he fled to America.

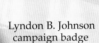

Lyndon B. Johnson campaign badge

LYNDON B. JOHNSON (1908–1973)
Johnson feared being the president who let Vietnam become Communist. He is seen, below right, with advisors aboard the presidential plane, Air Force One, flying back from meeting South Vietnamese leaders in Hawaii. Vice President Hubert H. Humphrey (1911–1978) sits at far left.

"We have no ambition there for ourselves, we seek no wider war."

LYNDON B. JOHNSON, 17 FEBRUARY 1965

NIXON AND KISSINGER
President Richard M. Nixon (1913–1994), left, walks with special advisor Henry A. Kissinger (b. 1923) in 1972. They are discussing ongoing peace talks in Paris. Nixon was first elected in 1968. He and Kissinger chose to prolong the war rather than withdraw from Vietnam and admit defeat.

Saigon and Hanoi

FOR CENTURIES, HANOI WAS THE LEADING Vietnamese city. As the capital of French Indochina, Hanoi was a centre of Vietnamese political, cultural, and economic life. The Communists made the city the DRV capital in 1954, but South Vietnam's capital, Saigon, soon passed Hanoi in wealth and population. A major commercial centre, Saigon had long dominated southern Indochina's social and cultural life. As South Vietnam's military headquarters, Saigon boomed from American financial aid. Hanoi's streets were busy with bicycles and handcarts, but Saigon's roared with cars and motor scooters. Then, with war intensifying, many military vehicles appeared in both cities.

HANOI POLITICIANS
DRV prime minister Pham Van Dong (sitting at centre) attends a 1946 Hanoi government meeting. Communists dominated the government, and many young people were active in Communist youth organizations. Yet, not all North Vietnamese were Communists.

WOMEN HOME GUARDS
An official registers female members of the Hanoi home guard, who are joining the army in 1964. Women were a large part of the home guard, which helped protect the city in time of conflict. This often included operating anti-aircraft weaponry.

Hanoi

During the French colonial period, Hanoi was famous for its restaurants and stylish upper class. After independence, the Hanoi region became a manufacturing centre with first-rate schools and hospitals. Its several hundred thousand residents suffered many hardships in their struggle with France. Still, they fought on in the Vietnam War to unify their country.

TWO VIETNAMS
Saigon and Hanoi were the main Vietnamese population centres. As major seaport, Saigon was strongly influenced by cultures from other lands. Hanoi was influenced by the neighbouring giant, China.

North Vietnam
South Vietnam

Communist flag

Pushcart

HANOI IN PEACEFUL TIMES
Few North Vietnamese owned motorized vehicles when they prepared for independence in 1954. Bicycles and pushcarts crowded this Hanoi street, with tramlines in the centre and Communist flags hanging from windows. Hanoi would soon be on its way to becoming a centre for government, industry, and higher education.

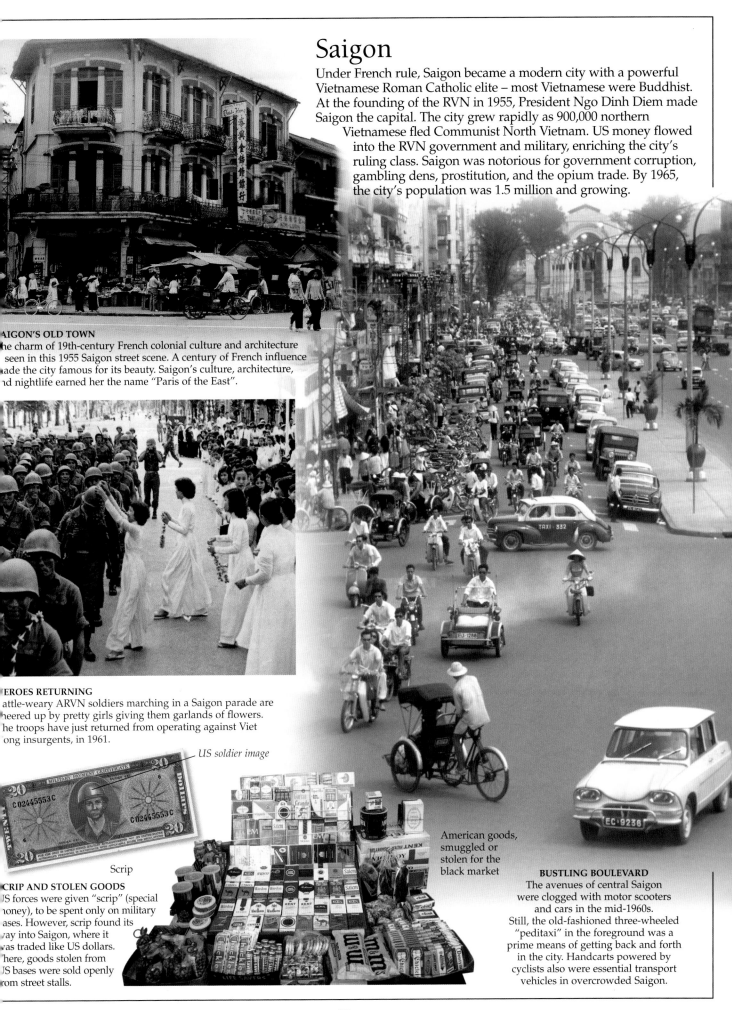

Saigon

Under French rule, Saigon became a modern city with a powerful Vietnamese Roman Catholic elite – most Vietnamese were Buddhist. At the founding of the RVN in 1955, President Ngo Dinh Diem made Saigon the capital. The city grew rapidly as 900,000 northern Vietnamese fled Communist North Vietnam. US money flowed into the RVN government and military, enriching the city's ruling class. Saigon was notorious for government corruption, gambling dens, prostitution, and the opium trade. By 1965, the city's population was 1.5 million and growing.

SAIGON'S OLD TOWN
The charm of 19th-century French colonial culture and architecture is seen in this 1955 Saigon street scene. A century of French influence made the city famous for its beauty. Saigon's culture, architecture, and nightlife earned her the name "Paris of the East".

HEROES RETURNING
Battle-weary ARVN soldiers marching in a Saigon parade are cheered up by pretty girls giving them garlands of flowers. The troops have just returned from operating against Viet Cong insurgents, in 1961.

US soldier image

Scrip

SCRIP AND STOLEN GOODS
US forces were given "scrip" (special money), to be spent only on military bases. However, scrip found its way into Saigon, where it was traded like US dollars. There, goods stolen from US bases were sold openly from street stalls.

American goods, smuggled or stolen for the black market

BUSTLING BOULEVARD
The avenues of central Saigon were clogged with motor scooters and cars in the mid-1960s. Still, the old-fashioned three-wheeled "peditaxi" in the foreground was a prime means of getting back and forth in the city. Handcarts powered by cyclists also were essential transport vehicles in overcrowded Saigon.

Rolling Thunder

THE TONKIN GULF INCIDENT and Viet Cong clashes with US troops convinced LBJ's national security advisors that North Vietnam must be punished. Key advisor McGeorge Bundy believed that bombing the North would prove that the United States was determined to defend South Vietnam. The Operation Rolling Thunder bombing campaign began in March 1965. It targeted bridges, motorways, railways, airfields, factories, power plants, and fuel depots. Johnson called a temporary halt to the bombing seven times. He hoped halts would give the Communists a chance to ask for peace terms. They did not. Despite the damage, the Hanoi government continued its war effort and kept the supply chain to the VC flowing. Johnson ordered an end to the campaign on 31 October 1968.

McGEORGE BUNDY (1919–1996)
Bundy was a security advisor to Presidents Kennedy and Johnson. He urged the bombing campaign and helped plan it.

AIR FORCE THUNDERCHIEFS
Air Force F-105 Thunderchief fighter-bombers are refueled in the air while on their way to bomb North Vietnam, in 1966. The refueling aircraft, at right, is a KC-135 Stratotanker. Many US fighter-bombers flew from bases thousands of kilometres away and had to refuel during their missions.

Stratotanker's drogue (refuelling device) connects with fighter-bomber to pump in fuel

389th Tactical Fighter Squadron patch

CHINA

NORTH VIETNAM — Hanoi

Haiphong

LAOS

Gulf of Tonkin

From Thailand

From S. Vietnam

B-52s from Okinawa

B-52s from Guam

Demilitarized Zone (DMZ)

US 7th Fleet

THAILAND

SOUTH VIETNAM

STRATEGIC TARGETS
Around 600,000 tonnes of bombs were dropped on North Vietnam during Rolling Thunder, causing great destruction. US aircraft avoided hitting major population areas around Hanoi and Haiphong, shown circled. LBJ wanted to minimize civilian casualties.

Chinese buffer zone (prohibited to US aircraft)

Target restrictions around Hanoi and Haiphong

US air attacks

SUCCESSFUL MISSION
Air Force commander George Jacobsen Jr signals with the "okay" sign that he has completed a mission against NVA ammunition depots in 1965. Jacobsen had just landed safely on the carrier USS *Ranger*, operating off the Vietnamese coast. US planes were limited to destroying military and economic targets during Rolling Thunder.

A-1 Skyraider warplane

Ammunition belt

Pilot helmet

OMBS FALL
-105 Thunderchiefs following a
-66 Destroyer over North Vietnam
lease their bombs. These small
ghter-bombers attacked targets with
reat accuracy, while high-flying
eavy bombers dropped payloads
ver a wider area. Fighter-bombers
ew low to avoid NVA radar. Radar
an electronic system that sends out
dio waves to detect objects at a
istance. Planes flying lower than
e radio waves are not detected.

AFTER A STRIKE
A North Vietnamese railway
bridge has partially collapsed
after a US air strike. Cutting
railroads made it difficult for
the Communists to transport
equipment and troops.
Whenever LBJ called a halt
to bombing, the North
Vietnamese hurried to rebuild
their damaged factories and
transport links.

*Bridge collapsed from
precision bombing*

Wild Weasel
patch

*Parachute
slows plane*

WILD WEASEL LANDING
This F-100 fighter's landing is slowed
by a tail parachute. The aircraft is
fitted with radar-jamming
equipment that interferes with
anti-aircraft electronic
devices. Nicknamed "Wild
Weasels", these fighters
specialized in finding and
attacking surface-to-air
missile (SAM) sites. They
flew daringly low, through
enemy fire, leading warplanes
into action against North
Vietnamese anti-aircraft positions.

North Vietnam's air defence

With aid from the USSR and China, Hanoi built a formidable
anti-aircraft defence. The small North Vietnamese Air Force also
became increasingly effective during Rolling Thunder. Most of
North Vietnam's warplanes and anti-aircraft weapons were provided
by its allies – as was training in their use and maintenance. During
Rolling Thunder, more bombs were dropped on North Vietnam than
the United States used in the Pacific Theatre in World War II.

HOME GUARD
Young women in the
Hanoi home guard
search the skies for
US warplanes.
Thousands of
civilians were
equipped with
weapons and
instructed to fire into
the air. This created a
storm of bullets to
drive off or
shoot down
an attacker.

HANOI POSTCARD
The Hanoi government
used postcards as
propaganda tools. This
card shows a peasant
watching a stricken
US aircraft flaming
to the ground. The
pilot has parachuted
clear, but will
be captured.

Greeting from
VIETNAM

THE VOICE OF VIETNAM
56-58 QUAN SU STREET — HANOI

Explosive warhead

AIMING A SAM
A surface-to-air guided missile crew on the outskirts of
Hanoi prepares for a US air attack. Thousands of
trained Chinese SAM operators volunteered
to serve in North Vietnam. SAMs were
more than 9 m (30 ft) long, with
114 kg (250 lb) of explosives. The
US campaign lost 922 aircraft, most
of them shot down by SAMs
and anti-aircraft guns.

Machine gun

Concrete rim

AIR-RAID ALARM
A Hanoi resident takes cover
n an air-raid shelter dug
nto the edge of a city street.
Wailing sirens alerted people
o find shelter immediately
whenever US planes were
earby. A piece of sheet
metal is at hand, to be
drawn over the hole for
cover if bombs fall.

Sheet metal cover

The Ho Chi Minh Trail

THIS NETWORK OF WILDERNESS ROUTES – named after Vietnam's nationalist hero – carried Communist equipment, supplies, and troops to fight in South Vietnam. The trail started near Hanoi, but was chiefly outside both Vietnams. The main trail wound into Laos, while another branch came through Cambodia. Many branches led into the South. Long sections passed through jungles that sheltered the trail from Allied bombing attacks. Anti-aircraft batteries were placed along the way, and there were underground barracks, hospitals, workshops, and storage areas for munitions and fuel. Supplies moved by foot, bicycle, and even elephant. The network grew to 20,000 km (12,500 miles) of trails and roads. Much of it was paved for truck traffic. Late in the war, 5,000 km (3,000 miles) of pipeline carried fuel over mountains and under rivers. By 1970 more than 18,000 tonnes of supplies moved on the trail every month.

MUSCLE AND STEEL
NVA engineers fight rushing waters to lay steel girders for a new bridge in 1966. Footpaths and river fords were gradually replaced with roads and bridges for trucks. Much of the trail was designed and built by the NVA's Logistics Group 559. This unit gained international recognition for its work. More than 100,000 Vietnamese worked to build and maintain the trail.

STAIRWAY TO WAR
NVA troops carefully walk down steep wooden steps set against a mountain cliff. This unit is journeying near the DMZ in 1966. It will need two months to complete its march to a final position in South Vietnam. The Ho Chi Minh Trail was also referred to as the "Truong Son Road", because it entered the Truong Son Mountains of central Vietnam.

VAST ROUTE
Parts of the Ho Chi Minh Trail passed through Laos and Cambodia. Both stayed neutral during the war. Cambodia's Prince Norodom Sihanouk dared not block the trail, fearing this would anger the Communists. Because he left the southern part of the trail alone, it was nicknamed "Sihanouk Trail".

**Map labels:**

NORTH VIETNAM
Demilitarized Zone (DMZ)
LAOS
Hué
Da Nang
THAILAND
CAMBODIA
Central Highlands
Mekong River
Phnom Penh
SOUTH VIETNAM
Saigon
Mekong Delta
Sihanoukville
South China Sea

▬▬ Ho Chi Minh Trail
▬▬ Sihanouk Trail

BICYCLE WARFARE
Transport labourers on the Ho Chi Minh Trail use heavily loaded bicycles to haul ammunition for NVA troops in 1967. The bikes are fitted with specially designed handles for easier steering while being pushed along. The Communists could not have waged war without the trail to move supplies.

Specially adapted handles

SULPHUR DRUGS
Protecting the health of thousands of transport labourers, soldiers, and engineering corps workers was an essential task for the NVA. This Russian-made container for sulphur drugs was used by the North Vietnamese. Sulphur was for treating infection from parasites or bacteria, and for malaria.

VIET CONG SANDALS
While US and ARVN soldiers had heavy boots and modern gear, Communist guerrillas used what they could salvage or make themselves. These sandals were cut from old rubber tyres and tied with leather straps.

IN RAINY MOUNTAINS
Communist troops trekking on the trail toward South Vietnam cross misty mountains near the Laos–North Vietnam border. As many as 20,000 NVA troops moved southwards on the Ho Chi Minh Trail every month. Many soldiers and labourers died on the way, from air raids, disease, snakes – and even tigers.

CHINESE TELEPHONE
Communications on the trail depended on field telephones, such as this Chinese instrument captured from the VC by US troops. Phones were installed at strongpoints or bunkers along the trail and linked by telephone cable.

1.5-volt dry-cell battery for power

Trees destroyed by US bombing and defoliation campaigns

ROAD FOR TRUCKS
Supply trucks pass through a crossroads in a defoliated part of the trail in the 1970s. By this time, trucks were the heart of the transport system, carrying troops as well as supplies. NVA engineering battalions worked mainly by hand at first. They later received earthmoving and roadbuilding equipment from the Soviets and Chinese.

Napalm and Agent Orange

EARLY IN THE VIETNAM WAR, US leaders called for eliminating the Viet Cong's support network in the countryside. This meant destroying food supplies and shelter, and driving out peasants who aided the VC. The military began to ruin vast areas of jungle and croplands by "defoliation" – killing all the leaves with chemical poisons. This exposed tree-covered guerrilla bases and supply routes to Allied aircraft. The weapons included "Agent Orange", a chemical defoliant sprayed over South Vietnam during a long-running air campaign. Also used were bombs containing napalm – an "incendiary" that burned all it touched. Defoliants and napalm turned once-beautiful and rich Vietnamese landscapes into wastelands.

WALTER W. ROSTOW
Top US advisor Walter Rostow (1916–2003) urged Kennedy and Johnson to destroy areas of VC support, leading to the use of deadly defoliants and napalm.

MAKING NAPALM
A US soldier mixes chemical thickeners in a drum of gasoline to make napalm, a jelly, in 1969. Upon exploding, flaming globules of napalm stick to everything the touch, causing great suffering. Flaming napalm also removes oxygen from the air bringing injury and death to victims, who are unable to breathe.

DESTRUCTIVE PAYLOAD
Napalm bombs are mounted under the wing of an Air Force F-4 fighter-bomber at Da Nang airfield. Napalm was first used in World War II and set entire cities ablaze.

Napalm explosion

NAPALM EXPLOSIONS
Liquid fire blossoms into fireballs as a napalm strike from the air blasts a remote VC hamlet into ashes in 1965. The clinging flame of a napalm attack burn for hour afterward on trees and buildings. Napalm was a US weapon of destruction widely used throughout the Vietnam War.

Ranch Hand's chemical assault

Operation Ranch Hand was the Air Force name for a campaign of spraying defoliants between 1962 and 1971. The defoliation squadron had just six aircraft at first, but grew to 25 by 1969. This was the peak of the campaign, which struck at VC bases in Cambodia as well as in South Vietnam. Streams of chemicals were sprayed on jungles and crop fields by slow-moving, low-flying, fixed-wing aircraft and helicopters. Most jungles could recover from two sprayings, but a third killed them. Mangrove swamps, however, died after only one spraying. More than 72 million litres (19 million gal) of herbicides were sprayed during the campaign – 60 percent of them Agent Orange.

The C-123 aircraft was most commonly used in Ranch Hand

Trail of defoliant spray

RANCH HAND PATCH
The 12th Air Command Squadron carried out Ranch Hand missions. Members wore this patch marking their participation.

BEFORE AND AFTER
The effects of Ranch Hand defoliation are seen in this aerial photograph of land that has been sprayed and land left untouched. The field on the right side of the river is brown after being poisoned with Agent Orange. The left bank is still lush green.

POISONOUS SPRAY
Low-flying aircraft spray herbicides over Communist-held country in Cambodia in 1966. Agent Orange can cause illness in humans. Both US service members and Vietnamese civilians have lasting health problems from contact with such herbicides.

HELICOPTER-BORNE HERBICIDE
A Huey helicopter sprays a defoliation agent over jungle in the Mekong Delta, in 1969. Here, the U Minh Forest of mangrove swamps had a dense canopy – treetops – that hid people and buildings from aircraft. Herbicides destroyed this canopy and exposed VC positions.

Machine gunner

RIVER THROUGH RUIN
A Vietnamese paddles his boat between the bare banks of a former mangrove forest in the Mekong Delta, in 1970. Agent Orange destroyed swamps that once were bountiful for fishing and agriculture.

Sampan propelled by oars

Central Highlands struggle

THE RUGGED MOUNTAINS BETWEEN Cambodia and the sea – Vietnam's Central Highlands – were fought over during the entire war. Strongholds of Viet Cong and NVA were attacked by US and Allied forces, but new ones soon arose. American bases in the region were under constant threat. Troops operating in the densely forested mountains could expect frequent ambushes. The Communists positioned soldiers and supplies in the Highlands, with the plan to break through to the seacoast one day. This would cut South Vietnam off from its northern provinces, which the Communists could then capture. Major battles in the Ia Drang Valley and at Dak To defeated the Communists, delaying their plans. The Americans found allies in the Montagnard people of the Central Highlands. US Special Forces trained and armed the Montagnards, who proved especially brave.

CENTRAL HIGHLANDS
Central Highlands valleys could lead Communist forces down to the coast. Major battles were fought to control the Highlands, where US bases blocked enemy movements.

NVA forces

NVA troops occupied large areas of the Central Highlands. They were trained in wilderness fighting and could move swiftly and silently. The Communists usually chose the time and place of battle in the mountains. The Americans and ARVN, however, won the major engagements during most of the war.

Communist star

NVA HELMET.
North Vietnamese soldiers wore cool and comfortable uniforms, with light but sturdy helmets that protected the wearer from sun and rain.

Strap

NGUYEN CHI THANH
General Thanh planned a major NVA offensive through the Central Highlands in 1965. His forces attempted to drive towards the sea, but they were defeated in battles in the Ia Drang Valley.

TUBULAR SCARF
The NVA soldier's daily ration of rice – his basic food – was carried in a hollow, tube-like scarf. Tied into a pouch, the scarf kept the rice secure.

Double spout

NVA OIL CAN
This two-compartment can held oil used to maintain weaponry.

AMMO POUCH
This ammunition belt with a harness is typical NVA "webbing", the term for military belts and pouches made of fabric. It holds three ammunition clips – magazines – and has pouches for bullets or tools.

Fastening loop

Ammunition clip

NVA CANTEEN
Communist fighters carried very little gear compared to heavily equipped US and ARVN troops. The outgunned Communists had to travel fast and live off the land. A canteen for water was one of the most essential pieces of equipment.

Harness strap

Elite forces and allies

US "Green Beret" Special Forces were active in the Central Highlands. Operating in small teams, they used guerrilla tactics against the NVA and made loyal allies of the native Montagnard peoples. The Montagnards (French for "mountain dwellers") were fiercely independent. They first opposed the South Vietnamese government, but the Special Forces arranged an alliance. Green Beret units equipped and trained the Montagnards and led them in battle. Other elite US forces fighting in the Central Highlands included the troopers of the Air Cavalry (Air Cav) and Airborne. When the Special Forces camp at Dak To was threatened by the NVA in 1967, these troopers led the counterattack that defeated the Communists.

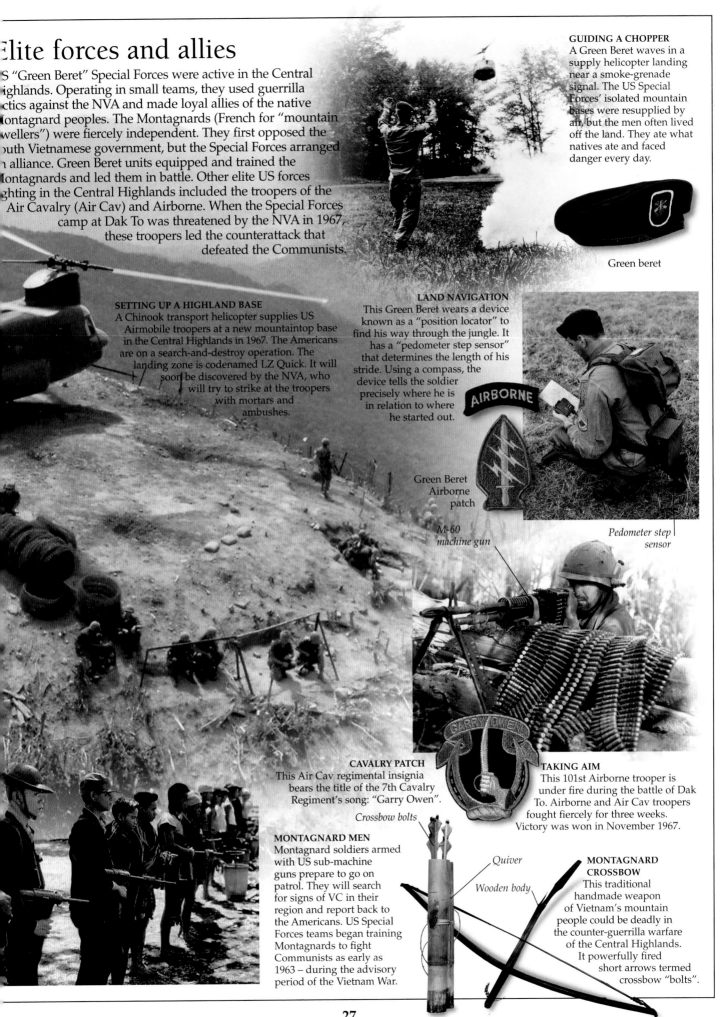

GUIDING A CHOPPER
A Green Beret waves in a supply helicopter landing near a smoke-grenade signal. The US Special Forces' isolated mountain bases were resupplied by air, but the men often lived off the land. They ate what natives ate and faced danger every day.

Green beret

SETTING UP A HIGHLAND BASE
A Chinook transport helicopter supplies US Airmobile troopers at a new mountaintop base in the Central Highlands in 1967. The Americans are on a search-and-destroy operation. The landing zone is codenamed LZ Quick. It will soon be discovered by the NVA, who will try to strike at the troopers with mortars and ambushes.

LAND NAVIGATION
This Green Beret wears a device known as a "position locator" to find his way through the jungle. It has a "pedometer step sensor" that determines the length of his stride. Using a compass, the device tells the soldier precisely where he is in relation to where he started out.

AIRBORNE

Green Beret Airborne patch

Pedometer step sensor

M-60 machine gun

CAVALRY PATCH
This Air Cav regimental insignia bears the title of the 7th Cavalry Regiment's song: "Garry Owen".

Crossbow bolts

TAKING AIM
This 101st Airborne trooper is under fire during the battle of Dak To. Airborne and Air Cav troopers fought fiercely for three weeks. Victory was won in November 1967.

MONTAGNARD MEN
Montagnard soldiers armed with US sub-machine guns prepare to go on patrol. They will search for signs of VC in their region and report back to the Americans. US Special Forces teams began training Montagnards to fight Communists as early as 1963 – during the advisory period of the Vietnam War.

Quiver

Wooden body

MONTAGNARD CROSSBOW
This traditional handmade weapon of Vietnam's mountain people could be deadly in the counter-guerrilla warfare of the Central Highlands. It powerfully fired short arrows termed crossbow "bolts".

Weapons of war

THE GROUND WAR IN VIETNAM was waged with many different weapons. Some were sophisticated and devastating, while others were primitive but deadly. Modern US firearms were matched by weaponry provided to the Communists by the Soviets and Chinese. The Communists also used an ancient method: booby traps set on jungle trails. The support of villagers was essential to Viet Cong resistance in South Vietnam. Women helped make booby traps, and men repacked spent shell casings to make explosive mines. For all the power of US Air Force bombing, the war was decided by ground action between foot soldiers. These bitter close-combat engagements required fierce courage on both sides.

CLAYMORE MINE
The US-made Claymore antipersonnel mine fired 700 steel balls 90 m (100 yd) in a 60-degree arc. The VC used captured Claymores against US troops.

NVA GUN
South Vietnamese militiamen captured this 75-mm recoilless rifle from NVA troops.

NVA and VC forces

The Soviet Union and China provided North Vietnam with great quantities of arms and also sent instructors to teach their use. We armed NVA troops controlled portions of South Vietnam and operated in fairly large units. The VC, however, moved in small u in the shadow of US and ARVN forces. VC often had to use weapo captured from their enemies. The captured Claymore antiperson mine was one of the deadliest weapons used in VC ambushes.

BOMB-MAKING
VC soldiers salvage US shell casings and unexploded artillery ammunition found on battlefields. Using hacksaws and grinding wheels, they reload the casings to make explosive devices. Grenades, above right, were also used in booby traps.

Grenades

Communist star

NVA knife

Rocket exhaust vent

Telescopic sight

SOVIET-MADE AK-47
Rapid-firing AK-47 assault rifle were the most important firearms carried by Commu troops. Assault rifles gave individual soldiers tremendou firepower.

Ammunition magazine

SOVIET 7D GRENADE LAUNCHER
The shoulder-fired rocket-propelled grenade launcher ("RPG") can blast defences apart, and some warheads can penetrate armour. The RPG allows infantrymen to destroy armoured personnel carriers and attack tanks.

Warhead holds explosive

Rocket-propelled grenade

Sharpene bamboo

BAMBOO STAKES
Villagers, above, sharpen bamboo into punji stakes that were used in booby traps. One method, right, was to set punjis in pits and cover them over with branches and leaves. The covering gave way when stepped on, and the individual fell into the pit.

SKS SIMONOV CARBINE
Most SKS rifles were provided by China. The bayonet for this rifle could fold into a barrel support when the soldier fired lying down.

Trigger guard and magazine

Free World Forces

Soldiers of the Free World Forces used weapons similar to those of the Communists: assault rifles and grenade launchers. Although far better than the weaponry [th]e VC used, FWF weapons were matched by NVA arms. One [a]dvantage to Free World Forces was their artillery. For most [of] the war, the Communists had almost none in the field. [A]nother advantage was the FWF's [in]exhaustible supplies. The Communists [d]epended on the Ho Chi Minh Trail for [re]supply. Free World Forces had huge bases [o]n the South Vietnamese coast. FWF troops [in] battle were resupplied by transport [p]lanes and helicopters.

Flash hider

Launcher attached to end of barrel

M-1 bayonet

Grenade and adaptor for M-1 carbine

Grenade

M1 CARBINE
ARVN troops often were equipped with older US firearms, such as this M-1 carbine. In general, the smaller, lighter carbine was easier for the more slightly built Vietnamese to use. The M-1 had a bayonet and fired rifle grenades as well as bullets.

30-round magazine

Barrel of grenade launcher

Sight for grenade launcher

Handle for cleaning rod

[M]-16 CLEANING KIT
[Fi]rearms must be perfectly maintained [(cl]eaned and oiled) or they may not [fir]e. This US M-16 cleaning kit [in]cludes brushes to swab the [in]side of the rifle barrel.

Cleaning fluid

Cleaning brush attaches to rod

Hinge to fold rod compactly into a pouch

Cleaning brush

M-16 bayonet

Bayonet sheath

US ASSAULT RIFLE
The M-16A1 offers more than the M-16 assault rifle's burst of automatic fire and 30-round magazine. The M-16A1 has a grenade launcher fixed under the muzzle. There is a separate sight and trigger for the grenade launcher. The combination offers greatly increased firepower in one weapon.

Sight

[U]S GRENADES
[In]fantry carried two or three grenades, which were [th]rown at the enemy and exploded. The ring for [th]e pin was pulled, and after the soldier threw the [g]renade a fuse began to burn down. In a few seconds, the grenade exploded.

Front sling fitting

Pineapple grenade

Baseball grenade

Lemon grenade

Ring is pulled before throwing

GRENADE LAUNCHER
This US M-79 grenade launcher, nicknamed "Blooper", has a range of 46–274 m (50–300 yd). This shoulder-fired weapon's grenade sends 300 metal fragments over an area 5 m (15 ft) in diameter.

Rear sling fitting

M-60 MACHINE GUN
A US Special Forces soldier fires an M-60 7.62-mm machine gun at enemy positions. This belt-fed "general purpose" machine gun was one of the most important weapons available to American forces in Vietnam. It was used extensively to support small-unit operations and was also mounted on helicopters.

[1]55-MM HOWITZER
[A]RVN artillerymen fire a 155-mm howitzer in the Central [H]ighlands. Shells from a howitzer follow a high trajectory [a]nd drop onto enemy positions. Defences that resist direct [f]ire can be vulnerable to shells dropping down from above.

On patrol

THE US MILITARY HAD ADVANCED WEAPONRY and powerful aircraft, but fighting in Vietnam required foot soldiers on patrol. Small groups of soldiers walked through dangerous areas known to have Communist activity. They patrolled rural villages where the people wanted protection from the Viet Cong or NVA. In these situations, patrols were often watched by hidden VC or NVA waiting for a chance to strike. Most patrols conducted "reconnaissance" (going out to learn the strength and location of enemy units). Reconnaissance patrols were usually in platoon or company strength of between 20 to 100 men, and went short distances. Patrols also might be part of a larger "search-and-destroy" mission, which tried to find Communists and kill or capture them. If a gun battle began, a patrol's commander radioed the base for air or artillery support, or reinforcement by helicopter.

TAKING BEARINGS
An infantryman on patrol in unfamiliar territory uses a compass to determine his location. The Lensatic military compass has a front sight and a magnifying lens. The magnifier shows the compass dial's bearing when he sights on an object – perhaps a tree or a building. The compass folds into a carrying case.

Sighting wire, used with rear-sight slot and lens to sight on objects

Rear-sight slot

Lens is used to magnify dial

Insect repellent

JUNGLE BOOTS
Waterproof boots were needed for patrolling in swampy jungles.

Waterproof material

INFANTRY HELMET
The soldier's helmet strap was convenient for holding a pack of Army-issue cigarettes and bug repellent.

Grenade

Collapsible shovel

Food pouch

Canteen

Ammo pouch

Smoke grenade

M18 SMOKE VIOLET

Bayonet in scabbard

DAY-PACK EQUIPMENT
This equipment belt with chest-wrap was used for a daytime patrol. It holds a shovel, a bayonet, grenades, a canteen, a first-aid kit, and pouches for food, gear, and ammunition. Fully loaded, it weighs 27 kg (60 lb).

Ammo pouch

Short-range antenna

Radio controls

Long-range antenna

PRC 9 backpack field radio

COLLECTING WATER
A 1st Infantry Division soldier on patrol refills his canteen at a flowing stream. Small 1.25-litre (2-pint) canteens were used on short patrols, while 5-litre (8-pint) canteens were used on long-range patrols. Water was made safe to drink by adding halazone, a powder that killed bacteria.

CALLING THE BASE
A radioman, left, carries a backpack field radio while his commanding officer uses the handset to report to headquarters. Patrols usually set out from fire bases – fortified encampments with headquarters, artillery, and support troops. A patrol could radio the base for VC or NVA positions to be shelled, or to request reinforcements or medevacs (medical evacuations).

Handset (phone)

Five-litre inflatable canteen

Vial of halazone water purifier

Instructions for inflating canteen

VC ambush

The Viet Cong were skilled at laying ambushes for approaching patrols. They hid in trees, in fields, and even underground. They often struck from all sides with a hail of gunfire and grenades. The leading man of the patrol – the soldier on point – was in particular danger from a surprise attack. If outnumbered, ambushers would soon melt into the countryside. If superior in force, they would try to wipe out the patrol before air support arrived.

IN THE OPEN
Troops of the 9th Infantry Division turn towards possible enemy movement as they walk across a rice paddy. Patrols were exposed to surprise attacks, especially as they entered forests, approached villages, or crossed open fields. This is a "day patrol", since the soldiers carry little gear or supplies. "Long-range reconnaissance patrols" went into the field for several days, often as part of search-and-destroy operations.

WATCHING AND WAITING
A VC fighter lies in a forest ditch, rifle at the ready. He is part of a force waiting silently to ambush a US or ARVN patrol.

DEMONSTRATING TACTICS
Posing for the camera, NVA troops show how to hide under haystacks. In combat, they would withdraw completely under the hay if an enemy patrol approached. If the patrol were too strong, the guerrillas would let it pass, hoping not to be discovered. Otherwise, they would attack on command.

Medical care and evacuation

As soon as the Vietnam conflict began, the American military rapidly expanded its medical service. In 1965, the United States had only two military hospitals in Vietnam, with 100 beds each. By 1969, there were approximately 30 US hospitals, with 5,000 beds, and two Navy hospital ships. These hospitals were staffed by 16,000 doctors, 15,000 nurses, and thousands of support personnel. On the battlefield, soldiers termed "medics" bandaged the wounded and called for helicopter airlifts. These emergency flights, known as "medevacs" (medical evacuations) quickly brought the injured to hospitals for immediate care. Communist field forces had primitive medical units. Their wounded were slowly carried to field hospitals hidden in swamps, caves, or tunnels.

MEDEVAC BUCKLE
"Dustoff" on this pilot's belt buckle is a nickname for ambulance helicopters, which landed and took off quickly.

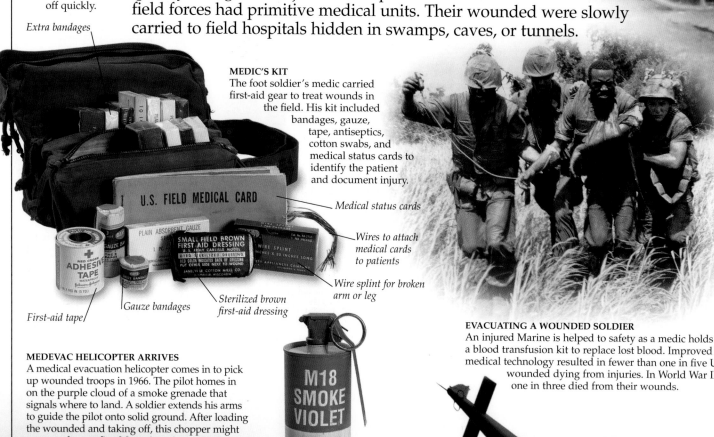

Extra bandages

MEDIC'S KIT
The foot soldier's medic carried first-aid gear to treat wounds in the field. His kit included bandages, gauze, tape, antiseptics, cotton swabs, and medical status cards to identify the patient and document injury.

U.S. FIELD MEDICAL CARD

Medical status cards

Wires to attach medical cards to patients

Wire splint for broken arm or leg

Sterilized brown first-aid dressing

Gauze bandages

First-aid tape

MEDEVAC HELICOPTER ARRIVES
A medical evacuation helicopter comes in to pick up wounded troops in 1966. The pilot homes in on the purple cloud of a smoke grenade that signals where to land. A soldier extends his arms to guide the pilot onto solid ground. After loading the wounded and taking off, this chopper might come under gunfire. Many Americans were treated within 20 minutes of being injured.

M18 SMOKE VIOLET

1701-9054

Purple smoke grenade

EVACUATING A WOUNDED SOLDIER
An injured Marine is helped to safety as a medic holds a blood transfusion kit to replace lost blood. Improved medical technology resulted in fewer than one in five US wounded dying from injuries. In World War II, one in three died from their wounds.

Rigid litter basket

BASKET FOR CASUALTIES
A US Army helicopter lowers a rigid litter basket to be loaded with a seriously wounded soldier in October 1967. Often, medical helicopters could not land in dense jungles that did not have clearings. Litters were lowered by steel cables, and the wounded were hauled up and swiftly flown away from the battlefield.

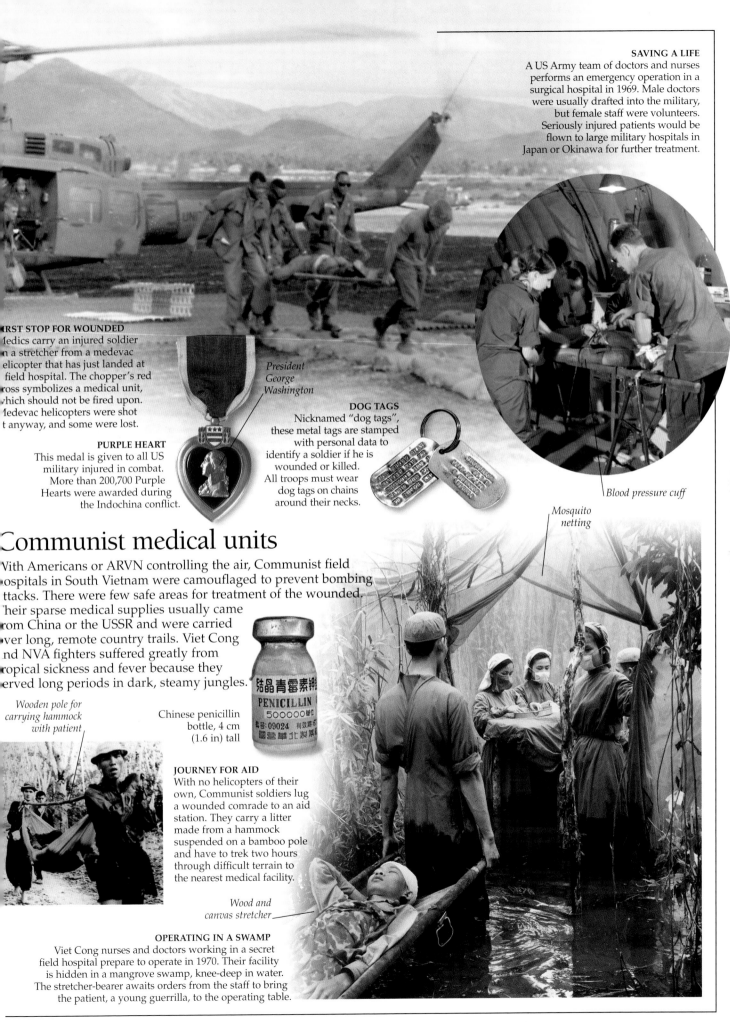

FIRST STOP FOR WOUNDED
Medics carry an injured soldier on a stretcher from a medevac helicopter that has just landed at a field hospital. The chopper's red cross symbolizes a medical unit, which should not be fired upon. Medevac helicopters were shot at anyway, and some were lost.

President George Washington

PURPLE HEART
This medal is given to all US military injured in combat. More than 200,700 Purple Hearts were awarded during the Indochina conflict.

DOG TAGS
Nicknamed "dog tags", these metal tags are stamped with personal data to identify a soldier if he is wounded or killed. All troops must wear dog tags on chains around their necks.

Blood pressure cuff

Mosquito netting

Communist medical units

With Americans or ARVN controlling the air, Communist field hospitals in South Vietnam were camouflaged to prevent bombing attacks. There were few safe areas for treatment of the wounded. Their sparse medical supplies usually came from China or the USSR and were carried over long, remote country trails. Viet Cong and NVA fighters suffered greatly from tropical sickness and fever because they served long periods in dark, steamy jungles.

Wooden pole for carrying hammock with patient

Chinese penicillin bottle, 4 cm (1.6 in) tall

結晶青霉素钾
PENICILLIN
500000单位
批号:09024 有效期至6
國营華北製藥廠

JOURNEY FOR AID
With no helicopters of their own, Communist soldiers lug a wounded comrade to an aid station. They carry a litter made from a hammock suspended on a bamboo pole and have to trek two hours through difficult terrain to the nearest medical facility.

Wood and canvas stretcher

OPERATING IN A SWAMP
Viet Cong nurses and doctors working in a secret field hospital prepare to operate in 1970. Their facility is hidden in a mangrove swamp, knee-deep in water. The stretcher-bearer awaits orders from the staff to bring the patient, a young guerrilla, to the operating table.

Heliborne warfare

MILITARY HELICOPTERS CAME INTO WIDE USE during the Vietnam War, termed the "Helicopter War". Until then, helicopters had been used only for scouting and for airlifting wounded. By the 1960s, US helicopters were redesigned with improved power and armaments. Nicknamed "choppers" because of their rotating blades, they rushed soldiers into action, fired at enemy positions, and transported equipment and supplies. Helicopters gave US and ARVN forces a great advantage because the NVA had no helicopters of their own.

HARRY W. O. KINNARD (b. 1915)
General Kinnard led the 1st Cavalry Division, which was the first military unit to be transported by helicopter. Known as "airmobile" or "heliborne" troops, Kinnard's division went to Vietnam in 1965.

M-16 rifle

Landing

Supply pouch

ROCKET ON TARGET
A rocket flashes from a US Navy helicopter, seen from above as it attacks an NVA position. This type of helicopter was nicknamed "Huey", after its model name: UH-1. Helicopter covering-fire supported ground troops, who communicated by radio to call in helicopters during combat.

AIR CAVALRY RIDE IN ON HELICOPTERS
Troopers of the 1st Air Cavalry Division hit the ground running as they jump down from a "Huey" helicopter during a scouting mission. "Air Cav" troopers were the world's first trained heliborne soldiers. Their success in Vietnam led to the widespread use of military helicopters and the creation of more airmobile units.

GUNNER DUTY
A machine gunner looks for Viet Cong while flying over South Vietnam. Helicopter gunners were favourite enemy targets. Their duty was considered one of the most dangerous of the war.

HUEY WEAPONRY
The Huey's armaments included seven-pod aerial-rocket launchers, on the right, and also rapid-firing machine guns, such as the "minigun" on the left.

Rockets

Machine gun ammunition belt

Helicopter wing

Helicopter landing wheel

Heavy machine gun

Fuselage and tail

Pilot and co-pilot positions

COBRA ATTACK HELICOPTER
This Marine Corps AH-1W Sea Cobra was one of the first models designed as an attack helicopter. The first AH-1s came into service in 1967. These "gunships" were specially built for escorting fast-moving transport helicopters. Although the heavily armed UH-1 Huey was the military's main workhorse helicopter, it was too slow to keep up with the transport helicopters. AH-1 Cobras were swift and manoeuvrable, with great firepower. They were employed by the Marines and the Army during the war.

Pilot and
co-pilot positions

Cannon

AIR CAVALRY INSIGNIA
Helicopter pilots and mechanics
wore patches that distinguished
them from the division's troopers.
These units of the 7th Squadron,
1st Cavalry Regiment, nicknamed
themselves "Apache Aeroscouts"
and "King Birds".

Apache Aeroscouts

King Birds

Cargo helicopters

The Americans and ARVN operated thousands of helicopters
during the war, with four main models: "utility" for general
use; "observation" for scouting; "attack" gunships for battle,
and "cargo" for transporting materials. The cargo helicopter
was needed everywhere, ferrying supplies and
equipment around the country. New models
had improved carrying-capacity, with more
powerful engines.

U.S. ARMY 03450

ARMY

CHINOOK AT WORK
The mighty CH-47 Chinook
helicopter was one of the best
cargo aircraft of the war. The
most frequently transported
freight of these heavy-lifting helicopters were field guns.
One such gun is shown suspended beneath the body
of a US Army Chinook, in flight to a distant base.

Landing wheel

Cannon barrel

Cannon limber

Field cannon

FLYING CRANE
This CH-54A Skycrane transport helicopter was
termed a "Flying Crane" for its ability to lift heavy
equipment and weapons. Loads were carried
in the cutaway under the fuselage. The Skycrane
often moved guns and vehicles into isolated
bases, where soldiers built fortifications
and artillery positions to
prepare for battle.

Rotors

Tail-mounted rotor

UNITED STATES ARMY 18411

Cutaway design
for large cargo

Tall landing
gear for cutaway

Warplanes in combat

THE "ROLLING THUNDER" BOMBING campaign struck North Vietnamese roads, railways, and bridges. This slowed the movement of Communist military supplies. Bombing population centres was not permitted, though, because LBJ did not want civilian casualties. This was why he did not use high-altitude heavy bombers that would cause widespread destruction. Most missions were carried out by F-105 fighter-bombers. These flew lower and were easier targets for anti-aircraft fire. By the end of 1966, 455 US warplanes had been shot down. The small North Vietnamese Air Force (NVAF) steadily improved. Its high-speed Soviet-made MiG-21 "interceptors" had downed 10 bombers and damaged many others. In January 1967, superior US fighters won a dramatic victory over the MiG-21s. By the end of 1967, the bombing campaign had devastated North Vietnam, but 649 US aircraft had been lost.

FIGHTER PILOT
The glow of the instrument panel lights the face of a US F-4 fighter pilot. He is preparing to take off on a night mission from Da Nang air base.

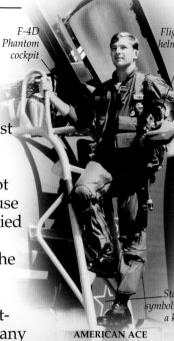

F-4D Phantom cockpit

Flig helm

Sta symbol a k

AMERICAN ACE
Captain Charles B. DeBellevu was the war's top US fighter pilot, or "ace". He flew 220 combat missions and won his title by shooting down six MiG

Tricking NVAF defenders

The NVAF's MiG-21s took on the less-manoeuvrable F-105 fighter-bombers but avoided the faster F-4 Phantoms. On 2 January 1967, Colonel Robin Olds led his 8th Tactical Fighter Wing in "Operation Bolo". Intending to draw MiG-21s into action, his F-4 fighters flew in the same formation, speed, and altitude as F-105 fighter-bombers. They also used F-105 radio call-signs. MiG-21s rose and were surprised to find themselves facing F-4 Phantoms. Seven MiG-21s were shot down, with no American losses.

US Air Force symbol on aircraft

Fuselage

Colonel's eagle

Rear horizontal wing stabilizes plane

Harness for parachute

Air-to-a missile

Vest with pouches

Inflation hose controls air pressure in flight suit

Flight suit

OPERATION BOLO LEADER
Colonel Robin Olds commanded the 8th Tactical Fighter Wing. He shot down one of the seven MiG-21s destroyed over North Vietnam during Operation Bolo. Olds eventually shot down four enemy aircraft. He earned the Air Force Cross, right, awarded for extraordinary heroism.

Air Force Cross

Bald eagle symbolizes America States and air striking power.

MIG-KILLERS
F-4 Phantoms fly in close formation while on patrol over Southeast Asia in 1967. This formidable fighter escorted the older and less manoeuvrable F-105 fighter-bombers in bombing missions over North Vietnam. The F- was the best fighter of the day, flying at speed of 2,500 kph (1,600 mph). They were termed "MiG killers". A total of 42 F-4s were lost in the Vietnam War.

DOGFIGHT
...ewed through the 20-mm cannon sight ...a pursuing F-105, a MiG is hit on the ...ng. The older F-105 fighter-bombers ...re often at a disadvantage to NVAF ...IGs in aircraft-to-aircraft ...gagements known as "dogfights". ...is F-105 next passed 7 m ...0 ft) beneath the ...omed MiG.

20-mm cannon sight

Second cockpit for weapons-system officer

Pilot's cockpit

Engine exhaust

M-61A1 20-mm cannon

Nose

NVAF ACE
Pham Thanh Ngan was the fourth-leading NVAF ace, having shot down eight US warplanes. He wears an Air Medal for each kill. NVAF pilots were trained by China and the USSR and flew aircraft made by those countries. Ngan flew a Soviet MiG-21, the best NVAF fighter.

Air Medal

Ho Chi Minh

AIR MEDAL
NVAF pilots received this medal for shooting down Allied aircraft.

PREPARING FOR TAKEOFF
In the cockpit of his MiG-21, third-best NVAF ace Mai Van Cuong readies for a mission. Cuong recorded eight kills, while the top NVAF ace, Nguyen Van Coc, had nine. MiG-21s were flown by 12 of the 16 NVAF aces. A pilot is declared an ace after he has five kills. The NVAF's 16 aces accounted for 106 of the 169 US warplanes shot down in air-to-air combat.

MiG cockpit

Cockpit cover

AIR BASE
A ground crew services a fighter at a North Vietnamese airfield on the outskirts of Hanoi. Since US bombers stayed away from Hanoi's population areas, NVAF aircraft were based near the city to avoid being bombed.

Serial number

SOVIET MIG-21
This MiG-21 fighter ...s on exhibit at a museum ...n Hanoi. The MiG-21 was ...designed as a fast interceptor ...o pursue, catch, and drive off ...ttacking enemy aircraft. This ...ighly manoeuvrable fighter flew ...t 2,200 kph (1,385 mph) and was ...rmed with air-to-air missiles. It ...as a "short-range" fighter, meant ...or defensive missions close to its home ...ase. Between 1965 and 1973, US ...varplanes downed 68 MiG-21s. Few ...NVAF fighter pilots survived the war.

NVAF symbol on aircraft

Landing gear

The Television War

THE VIETNAM WAR WAS CALLED the first "Television War", because television brought the horrors of war into American homes as never before. News reporting influenced how Americans understood the war. At first, most US journalists working in Vietnam supported the war. They reported on the military situation but did not explain Vietnam's long struggle against foreign rule. As the conflict became worse, the US government pretended it was going well. Then some influential journalists, such as Walter Cronkite, turned against the war and called for peace negotiations. Meanwhile, the North Vietnamese press tried to influence world opinion to oppose the war.

AT THE TYPEWRITER
Reporter Neil Sheehan writes about the Vietnam conflict in 1963. Sheehan first reported for the news service United Press International (UPI) and then for *The New York Times*. He later exposed government lies about the war.

Bronze Star

News film camera

Microphone

Sound monitor

INTERVIEWING SOLDIERS
Reporters and cameramen from CBS television news interview US soldiers about a recent battle in 1967. American military commanders gave journalists in Vietnam considerable freedom to travel around and meet the troops.

FIGHTING REPORTER
UPI's Joseph Galloway often fought alongside the troops he covered. Galloway won a Bronze Star medal for carrying a wounded man to safety.

Helmet with AP logo

AIMING WITH A CAMERA
Vietnamese photographer Huynh Thanh My lies in muddy water under enemy fire while on assignment for the news service Associated Press (AP). My covered ARVN troops fighting in the Mekong Delta in 1965. He was killed later that year on a similarly risky assignment.

YOUNG PHOTOJOURNALIST
Twelve-year-old Lo Manh Hung checks his camera while taking pictures in Saigon, in 1968. At the age of 10, this Vietnamese youth began working with his father – a veteran photojournalist. Hung wears a military helmet – proof of the danger he often faced. His helmet is labeled with "Press" in both English and Vietnamese.

HELPING THE INJURED
In 1975 UPI photographer Willy Vicoy carries a wounded girl to safety after heavy rocketing near Cambodia's capital, Phnom Penh. A US Navy vessel has just transported the child and her family away from the bombing. Correspondents and photographers often put off covering events to take part in them, usually to help the injured or elderly.

Stars and Stripes correspondent patch

NEWS ABOUT HIS WAR
A 9th Division soldier reads the Army's daily newspaper, *Stars and Stripes,* which tells of military action and antiwar protests. This paper was respected for reporting what soldiers wanted to know about the war and politics.

PRESS PASS
MACV issued press cards to "war correspondents", as journalists were termed. Frances FitzGerald's reporting won her fame.

Department of Defence seal

NVA PRESS CONFERENCE
Viet Cong general Tran Van Tra holds a press conference near the battlefront. Like the Americans and South Vietnamese, Communist officials strictly limited information about the war. Newspapers were the main North Vietnamese source of news. The nation's first television network, Vietnam Television, went into service in 1970.

PENTAGON CONFERENCE
US secretary of defence Robert McNamara faces microphones at the Pentagon in 1967 as he answers journalists' questions about the war. The government's daily press conferences often gave reporters overly optimistic or misleading reports. This caused many journalists to mistrust the information.

Map of Vietnam

WALTER CRONKITE AND VIETNAM
Highly respected CBS television anchorman Walter Cronkite reports on the Vietnam War in 1968. Cronkite dismayed many Americans by comparing the destruction and loss in the Vietnam conflict to World War II, which he had covered. Cronkite criticized US military policy, and LBJ grumbled, "If I've lost Cronkite, I've lost middle America."

EXPOSING THE TRUTH
In 1971, former Pentagon staffer Daniel Ellsberg gave *The New York Times* secret documents detailing government lies about the war. Neil Sheehan and other journalists reported on the documents in a series of articles titled "The Pentagon Papers". Most Americans were now convinced the war should be stopped.

CAMBODIA
Central
Highlands
SOUTH
VIETNAM
Phnom Penh
Mekong
River
Saigon
Bassac
River
Ap Bac
Ben Tre
Can Tho
Vinh Long
Ham Luong River
Co Chien River
Mekong
Delta
South China Sea

Areas of riverine
operations

MEKONG DELTA
The 4,500-km (2,800-mile) Mekong River deposits
fine soil as it empties into the South China Sea,
building up a delta (sandy lowland). Near
the Mekong Delta is Saigon, South Vietnam's
largest city. The areas shaded in blue on the
map show US and ARVN riverine operations
against the VC.

The Mekong Delta

THE MEKONG DELTA OF SOUTHERN VIETNAM is Indochina's
"rice bowl". Much of the delta is covered with waterlogged
paddies – fields of rice, the most important food in Asia. The
delta is at the mouth of the Mekong River and covers 67,340
sq km (26,000 sq miles). Crisscrossed by muddy channels and
streams, the delta was a guerrilla stronghold throughout the
Indochina wars. In the Vietnam War, US and ARVN forces
established military bases to control the delta's scattered
villages – often built on poles above the water. Gunboats
trying to find and destroy Viet Cong bases passed along
the waterways, while infantry patrolled on foot. Aircraft
scouted for the guerrillas, then struck at their positions
or supply routes. The VC retreated from superior
forces, but returned to fight again. They held on
throughout the war, aided by a population
that, for the most part, supported their cause.

STRIKE MISSION
Flames and smoke rise from a
rocket attack by an American UH-18
Iroquois helicopter in the Mekong
Delta. Twisting waterways and
patchwork rice paddies are
surrounded by dense woods that
shelter VC guerrillas.

Flames from
rocket strike

Swamp buffalo serve as draught
animals for rice cultivation

UNDER A GUN
An ARVN armoured personnel
carrier's heavy machine gun
aims at the Mekong Delta
horizon as a farmer ploughs his
rice paddy. The government
often destroyed rice crops in
order to keep VC guerrillas from
sharing farmers' food. Losing
their crops angered farmers, and
many turned against the
government to side with the VC.

VC FIGHTER
Guerrilla sentry Soc Trang stands a
her post in the Mekong Delta in 1973
Trang was only 24 years old bu
already had been widowed twice
Both husbands had been VC soldier
who died in action. The VC and North
Vietnamese forces counted man
women among their fighters bearin
arms in the field. Trang ha
a captured US M-16 rifle

MEKONG HAMLET
This view from a low-flying aircraft in 1968 shows a remote hamlet surrounded by the waters of the Mekong River. The river flows slowly here and is only about a metre deep beside the houses. Boats are the main form of transport, but houses are linked by built-up paths that have been used for centuries.

Path between houses

Thatched roof

POLING HOMEWARD
Mekong Delta family members use long poles to push a boat through the shallow waters that surround their hamlet. A neighbour building a new house works on the roof's ridgepole. The typical hamlet home is framed with poles that are covered with a thatched roof – usually a blanket of dried leaves or straw held down by rope and more poles. These houses stand on earthen bases above the water level.

Captured US M-16 rifle

Poles support racks for drying fishing nets

SOLDIER'S PATCH
This uniform patch is from the US 9th Infantry Division, which served in the Mekong. This was a difficult service, with frequent VC ambushes and a hot, steamy climate.

C131-2

MONITOR IN THE MEKONG
A heavily armed and armoured Monitor gunboat churns slowly past a large village in the Mekong Delta during an operation against the VC. The US Navy gunboat is heading for a nearby base, where other military craft are gathered to support the operation. The crewmen and soldiers of a US vessel docked just up ahead watch the gunboat approach.

War on inland waters

EARLY IN 1965, THE US NAVY BEGAN patrolling South Vietnam's 4,800 km (3,000 miles) of inland waterways. Many Vietnamese rivers, canals, and streams were narrow and jungle-covered, and Viet Cong ambushes made them dangerous to enter. In the swampy Mekong and Saigon river deltas, Communist forces dominated thousands of remote villages and farms. To penetrate these strongholds, MACV headquarters established a joint Army–Navy task force. In 1967, the Mobile Riverine Force – "riverine" means operating along waterways – went into action. It combined Army troops with the crews of fast Navy patrol boats, armoured gunboats and troop carriers, and napalm-firing boats. Larger vessels served as floating barracks that followed the action inland. Riverine units were nicknamed the "Brown Water Navy" since they operated in muddy waterways. The Brown Water Navy struck deep into enemy territory, opening much of the delta region to Saigon government control.

ELMO R. ZUMWALT JR (1920–2000)
Called the "Father of the Brown Water Navy", which he helped establish, Admiral Zumwalt commanded US naval forces in Vietnam from 1968 to 1970.

NAVAL PATCHES OF VIETNAM
Each naval unit had a distinctive uniform patch. Sailors of the USS *White River,* a World War II-era warship, wore a design with an eagle perched on an early naval cannon. Task Force 116, also called the River Patrol Force, wore a round patch with a shield, lightning bolts, and swords. River Assault Division 91 wore a patch showing a fighting "River Rat" riding a patrol boat.

River Assault Division 91 patch

USS *White River* naval patch

Patch of the River Patrol Force, Task Force 116

GUNBOAT IN THE MEKONG
A "Monitor" patrols the Mekong Delta near Saigon in 1967. These armoured vessels were named after Union gunboats of the US Civil War.

Frame for canvas roof

50-mm cannon

Reinforced steel hull

Rotating armoured gun turret

Loading ramp falls forward onto river bank when landing troops

PATROLLING THE MEKONG
A US Navy task force churns through the waters of the Viet Cong-held Mekong Delta in late 1967. These heavily armoured river assault boats were part of the joint Army-Navy Mobile Riverine Force. They are moving down a canal in one of several missions code-named Operation Coronado, which inflicted heavy losses on the enemy.

Thick steel armour protects troops

Pole used to propel craft and for steering

ARVN RIDE A SAMPAN
South Vietnamese troops, in the southern province of Ca Mau, South Vietnam, return to camp in a native craft loaded with firewood. South Vietnam had a modern navy, but its riverine forces often used the traditional sampan, powered by oars or by poling in shallow waters.

ZIPPO BLASTS ENEMY POSITIONS
The Navy's deadly flame boats were nicknamed "Zippos", after a popular brand of cigarette lighter. Guns on the Zippo's turrets shot streams of flaming napalm up to 180 m (200 yd), destroying everything within range. Napalm is a jelly that sticks to its target and keeps on burning. In ambushes, the Viet Cong often attacked the dangerous Zippos first to knock them out of action.

BURNING OUT VC
Primitive but effective, the flaming arrow being fired from this American officer's bow will set the straw roofs of a Viet Cong riverbank base on fire. Such strikes avoided the need to land troops.

Radar mast

Pilothouse

Deckhouse

SWIFT BOAT ON PATROL
A Navy Swift boat makes a high-speed run in South Vietnam's Cam Ranh Bay. The Swifts, officially termed "patrol craft fast" (PCF), served along the coast and on inland rivers. Each speedy Swift was mounted with a machine gun and an 81-mm mortar.

SHARK-MOUTHED HOVERCRAFT
Fiercely decorated, fast-moving patrol air cushion vehicles (PACVs) crossed swamps and waterlogged rice paddies where no other vehicle could go. These hovercraft transported troops for surprise assault missions and could move quickly to block enemy escape routes. This PACV's cushion of forced air lifts it across dry land.

Shark-tooth bow design

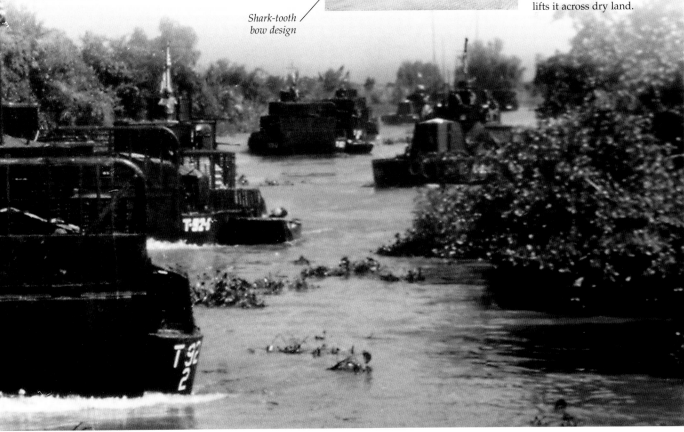

Villages in wartime

Rings of bamboo walls

VIETNAMESE PEASANTS IN THE COUNTRYSIDE lived much like their ancestors. The seasonal cycles of ploughing, planting, harvesting, and fishing shaped daily life – but war too often caused suffering. VC fighters depended on support from the villagers and threatened those who did not cooperate with them. US and ARVN troops, in turn, ordered villagers not to aid the VC. The Saigon government built defences and walls around some communities to keep VC out. Peasants tried to carry on farming, but soldiers of both sides often punished them for helping the opposition. In 1968, US troops massacred hundreds of civilians in the village of My Lai. When the news reached America, many more people turned against the war.

STRATEGIC HAMLETS
In the early 1960s, South Vietnam built fortified towns guarded by civilian militia, shown on the left. They were surrounded by fences and ditches, visible in this aerial view. Peasants were forced to move in to keep them from the VC. Yet most wanted to go home, and the programme ended after a few years.

Sharpened bamboo

COMING CLOSE
A US Army scout helicopter drops down low to investigate villagers tending buffalo in a meadow. ARVN troops are approaching in the background. Peasants never knew whether soldiers in passing helicopters would think they were VC and suddenly fire on them. Living in a combat zone exposed farmers to danger every day.

AFTER ACTION
ARVN soldiers talk with peasants in a rural village soon after an engagement with VC guerrillas. The soldiers had just fought off a VC ambush, and an ARVN lieutenant was killed. The officer's body lies in the bottom of the boat being poled into the village. If the soldiers think any of these villagers helped the VC, their huts will probably be burned.

ON TRIAL
A jungle village's "people's court" led by the VC tries a young man accused of aiding the ARVN. Villagers hear the charges before voting on a verdict. The youth was found guilty and sentenced to two years in prison. A companion put on trial along with him was sentenced to death.

PACIFICATION PROGRAMME
A Marine chaplain demonstrates a toy trumpet to Vietnamese children. Bringing toys, food, and humanitarian aid – such as medical care – was part of a relief programme organized by the United States known as the Pacification Programme. The military wanted to "win the hearts and minds" of the people by trying to earn their trust.

Dwellings

Shoulder basket

SEARCHING FOR COMMUNISTS
Air Cavalry troopers cautiously search a house for signs of NVA or VC soldiers. The troopers are on patrol in the rugged Central Highlands, where NVA troops operated in large numbers. The Air Cav has the mission to clear out the Communists, whose agents could be hiding among civilians.

CHORES IN A WAR ZONE
Peasant women carrying shoulder baskets meet US Marines assembling on a road. The women keep to the middle as the troops part to let them through.

Massacre at My Lai

Soldiers of the US Army American Division entered the hamlet of My Lai on 16 March 1968, with orders to burn it. The troops believed the villagers were VC sympathizers. Under the command of Lt William L. Calley Jr, they herded more than 300 men, women, and children together and shot them. Other villagers were saved when a US helicopter crew threatened to fire on Calley's men. The military tried to cover up the massacre but the story leaked out.

Several soldiers were tried for murder, but only Calley was convicted. He was immediately released on parole.

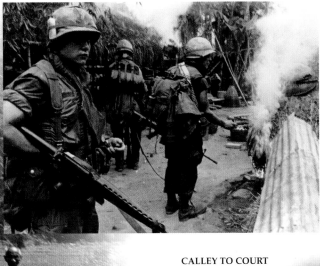

FIRE AND DEATH
After killing hundreds of civilians, Americal Division soldiers burn the hamlet of My Lai. There were no reports of the troops having come under attack. A year later, a former soldier wrote a letter to President Nixon, the Pentagon, and members of the US Congress about the atrocity, which became public. Many Americans were outraged, and the antiwar movement gained strength.

CALLEY TO COURT
William Calley, centre, and his military and civilian attorneys arrive for a pretrial hearing in Fort Benning, Georgia, in January 1970. A large number of Americans believed Calley should not have been punished because both sides had killed so many civilians. Calley was sentenced to life imprisonment, but President Nixon arranged to have the sentence reduced to 20 years. Later, Nixon granted Calley parole after the officer had spent only three days in a military jail.

Tunnels

THE VIETNAMESE BEGAN digging tunnels during the First Indochina War. These were used as bomb shelters and places for anti-French guerrillas to hide weapons. Tunnelling continued during the Vietnam War in Communist-controlled areas of South Vietnam. Guerrilla fighters and their supporters lived for long periods underground in complex tunnel systems. The largest networks included sleeping rooms, kitchens, ammunition depots, hospitals, and meeting halls. When US or Allied troops passed by, fighters hid in the tunnels or else came out for surprise attacks. Allied forces sent courageous volunteers, armed only with pistols and knives, into the tunnels to find out if they were being used.

VIET CONG DIG TUNNELS
Vietnamese labourers use primitive tools to hand-dig an entrance to a tunnel system. They lift out dirt-filled reed baskets, empty them, then send them back down for more. When completed, this part of the tunnel will be covered over, hidden from the surface.

Wooden plug   *Shrapnel pieces*

VC antipersonnel mine

Trigger mechanism

BOOBY TRAPS
The VC set traps to injure enemy troops coming into a tunnel. Traps included mines detonated by a trip wire, and even poisonous snakes, such as vipers or cobras. Snakes kept in bamboo stalks would be released if the stalks were accidentally knocked out of place by anyone crawling through.

Chinese cobra

TUNNELS AT CU CHI
The largest tunnel complex was at Cu Chi, 75 km (45 miles) north of Saigon. Here were more than 250 km (155 miles) of tunnels. This illustration, on display at the Cu Chi Museum's visitor centre, shows how many parts a tunnel system could have. They were several levels deep, with electricity, underwater entrances, air shafts, sentry posts, and a headquarters.

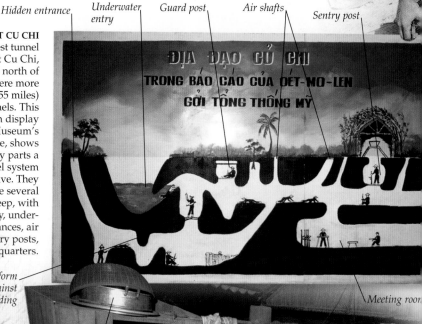

Hidden entrance   *Underwater entry*   *Guard post*   *Air shafts*   *Sentry post*

ĐỊA ĐẠO CỦ CHI
TRONG BÁO CÁO CỦA ĐẾT-MO-LEN
GỜI TỔNG THỐNG MỸ

Meeting room

SKS Simonov carbine

Airtight platform protects against flooding

Rice cooker

ON GUARD
A VC sentry waiting underground is alert for possible enemy discovery of his tunnel. The entrance to the tunnel is on the right.

Wood stoves

Cover over food keeps out bugs and rodents

UNDERGROUND KITCHEN
The cooking area of a tunnel mess hall was vented by shafts that sent smoke in many directions to make it unseen above ground. Some VC lived underground for months at a time and seldom saw sunlight. They would suddenly come out to make an attack and just as suddenly vanish into the tunnels before their enemies recovered.

Wash bucket

TURNING TUNNEL RAT

US soldier is pulled out of a tunnel
has just searched. In general,
[A]mericans were physically larger
[th]an Vietnamese and had trouble
[sq]ueezing through the narrow
tunnels. This man
wears a gas mask
and goggles against
tear gas he threw
into the tunnel
before entering.

Flak jacket

Gas mask

Torch

Tunnel rats

"Tunnel rats" were a special breed of soldier who took on one of
the most dangerous and frightening duties of the war. At first
termed "tunnel runners", they were extremely courageous
and daring. They risked their lives by crawling alone into
unexplored VC tunnels to find if they led to major
networks or supply centres. With only a pistol, knife, and
torch, they squirmed through twisting, dark tunnels.
They might meet a waiting enemy sentry or run into
a hidden booby trap – or might find nothing at all.

Pull-ring

GAS AND GAS MASK

Before entering a tunnel, a tunnel rat often
tossed in a tear-gas canister. He hoped any
enemy guards in there would be sickened
and forced away by the nauseating gas.
Wearing a gas mask so
he could breathe, the
soldier then
crawled into
the tunnel.

GAS
CN-DM

PB-2-68

Handle

Tear gas

Air filter

Tear gas mask

Strap

*Special
non-rolling design*

Belt clip

TUNNEL-RAT GEAR

[Th]e .45 pistol was
[th]e tunnel rat's most
[po]tent weapon, but he also
[ca]rried a "Ka-Bar" combat
[kn]ife. There were instances of
[m]en encountering enemies in the
[tu]nnels, and deadly shootouts
[re]sulted. Since tunnels were
[de]signed with many turns, bullets
[tra]velled only short distances
[be]fore hitting a wall.

.45 calibre bullet

.45 pistol

Bullet and
magazine

Torch

Hilt

Handle

Ka-Bar knife

Ka-Bar sheath

NO ROOM TO SPARE

A 173rd Airborne
Division engineer squats
with knife and pistol in a
tunnel 4.6 m (15 ft) below
the surface. He is in the
"Iron Triangle" region, a
VC stronghold north of
Saigon. His unit is
searching for VC
caches of food
and ammunition.

Khe Sanh and Tet

ON 21 JANUARY 1968, the Communists surprised the US Marine base camp of Khe Sanh with a storm of artillery fire. This opened General Giap's long-planned offensive that erupted all over South Vietnam on 30 January. The assaults began during the Vietnamese New Year, known as "Tet", when half the ARVN troops were home on leave. The Tet Offensive struck more than 100 cities and towns, even the centre of Saigon. Fighting raged for four weeks, inflicting heavy losses on the Communists, who were defeated. Yet Americans now knew the war had no end in sight.

YEAR OF THE MONKEY
The Vietnamese give each year a Chinese zodiac animal symbol, such as a snake or horse, and 1968 was the Year of the Monkey. According to the zodiac, the monkey is a creature that often desires revenge.

Khe Sanh

Khe Sanh's 6,000 Marines and ARVN troops blocked enemy supply routes from Laos. The Communist siege of the base in early 1968 was intended to draw other Allied forces away from the cities, which were soon attacked. Thousands of US and Allied troops battled to get through to the base, which gallantly held out for 77 days before being relieved.

LBJ STUDIES KHE SANH
President Johnson and advisors examine a scale model of besieged Khe Sanh. LBJ believed Giap wanted to turn Khe Sanh into another Dien Bien Phu. Such a defeat would force the United States to withdraw, as the French had in 1954. For two-and-a-half months, Americans anxiously followed the course of the siege.

TET OFFENSIVE
Bases and government buildings across South Vietnam were attack during Tet. Hué and Saigon came under the fiercest assaults.

US M-101 howitzer

KHE SANH ARTILLERY
American gunners at Khe Sanh reply to enemy artillery fire with their own bombardment. Marines and South Vietnamese allies fought hand-to-hand to drive off enemy infantry attacks. Each week, the defenders were hit with 2,500 rounds of Communist artillery, mortars, and rockets.

EXPLOSION AT KHE SANH
Marines duck as an ammunition storage pit takes a direct hit. Like Dien Bien Phu, Khe Sanh was surrounded by hills with Communist gun positions. The Americans, however, had overwhelming air power that blasted those guns. Also, helicopters braved hostile fire, bringing in supplies and evacuating wounded. Relief forces fought their way through on 8 April, finally ending the siege.

Battle sites
Areas of fighting
Ho Chi Minh Tra

Saigon

The most important struggle of the Tet Offensive was the battle for Saigon, South Vietnam's capital city. A team of 19 VC guerrillas broke into the US embassy compound and fought for several hours before being wiped out. The main event was the assault on MACV headquarters at Tan Son Nhut airfield. US and Allied forces led by General Frederick Weyand fought off every VC attack, defeating the enemy by 5 February.

FREDERICK C. WEYAND (b. 1916)
As commander of II Field Force (which defended Saigon), General Weyand received warnings of a coming major assault. He pulled his forces closer to Saigon to be ready. Weyand's success during Tet earned him eventual promotion to overall command in Vietnam.

South Vietnamese flag

Hué

Most Tet fighting ended in a few days, but the battle for Hué lasted until 2 March. Part of this ancient city had been the capital of imperial Vietnam. Fighting destroyed much of Hué and its Imperial Citadel, or fortress. Although the Communists lost Tet, they won a political victory: many more Americans opposed the war. Tet was the turning point of the Vietnam conflict, which increasingly favoured the Communists.

VIETNAMESE RANGER 35 BN

ARVN
Ranger patch

ARVN RETAKE CITADEL
Weary South Vietnamese troops have planted their flag on a tower of Hué's Citadel, shattered by a month of conflict. US and ARVN forces attacked VC and NVA fighters holding the walled fortress, and Allied warplanes and naval gunfire blasted enemy-occupied buildings.

SAIGON RECOVERS FROM TET
Saigon had seen little violence before Tet. Afterwards, residents had to pick their way through endless rubble to search for victims and clean up their homes.

VIET CONG IN HUÉ
As the battle rages, a VC radio operator sends messages to Communist troops in Hué. The radioman is in Hué's Imperial Citadel, which saw fierce fighting.

AFTER THE BATTLE
Members of the US 5th Marine Regiment patrol a war-torn street in Hué. These troops reinforced Allied units and fought for three brutal weeks to recapture the city. The destroyed Imperial Citadel is in the background.

49

The antiwar movement

Peace symbol

"V" peace sign

PEACE SIGNS
The peace symbol, top, appeared in early demonstrations against nuclear weapons. The *V* for victory became a sign of unity for antiwar Democrats in 1968.

BY 1965, MANY AMERICANS OPPOSED their government's involvement in Vietnam. That year, more than 20,000 antiwar demonstrators marched in Washington, DC. At first, the war's supporters and opponents took part in "teach-ins" to debate their positions peacefully. As the war worsened, opposition and demonstrations grew in size and anger. Hundreds of thousands gathered at major protests, where famous performers and political leaders spoke out against the war. President Johnson was so troubled by the widespread antiwar movement that he chose not to run for president in 1968. Hostility caused clashes between Americans for and against the war. In 1970, several college students were killed when soldiers in Ohio and police in Mississippi shot protesters.

A VOICE FOR PEACE
Folk singer Joan Baez joined leading antiwar musicians such as Pete Seeger, Phil Ochs, Bob Dylan, and the group Peter, Paul and Mary to entertain at peace demonstrations.

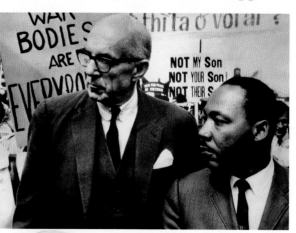

RESPECTED LEADERS
Famous baby doctor and author Benjamin Spock, far left, marches with civil rights champion Dr Martin Luther King Jr, near left, at a 1967 peace rally in Chicago. They led 5,000 people in the protest march, demanding an end to the Vietnam War. The influence of such highly regarded leaders convinced many Americans to oppose the war.

1969 Moratorium Against the War badge

FLOWERS INSTEAD OF BULLETS
In one of the most famous photographs of the antiwar movement, a demonstrator places carnations in the barrels of military police rifles. This incident occurred during a 1967 demonstration by more than 100,000 protesters at the Pentagon, headquarters of the Defence Department in Washington.

Tear gas canister

Tear gas mask

Launcher for tear gas canister

GAS, THEN BULLETS
Ohio national guardsmen fire tear gas at Kent State University demonstrators in May 1970. Troops also fired bullets that killed four students and wounded others. Some casualties were not protesters, but just students walking to class. The shootings sparked a nationwide student strike, closing hundreds of campuses. Two students at Jackson State College in Mississippi were also shot and killed, by police, later that month.

FIGHTING BACK
A protester in Berkeley, California, hurls a tear gas canister back at police who had fired it, in 1970. Tear gas briefly burned the eyes and throat, and forced most demonstrators to retreat.

US Capitol Building

North Vietnamese flag

Vietnam Veterans Against the War symbol

MARCH FOR A MORATORIUM ON THE WAR
In November 1969, huge demonstrations occurred all across America, urging an immediate moratorium – a temporary halt in the fighting. One march filled Pennsylvania Avenue, near the Capitol Building in Washington. Signs called for US troops in Vietnam to get "Out Now" and for the release of jailed antiwar activists. The main demonstrations were mostly peaceful, but afterwards some protesters battled with police.

VIETNAM VETERANS AGAINST THE WAR
Among the strongest opponents of the Vietnam conflict were soldiers who had served over there and considered the war wrong. Their main organization was Vietnam Veterans Against the War, shown marching in Miami Beach in 1972. Many antiwar veterans threw away their medals in protest.

Silver Star

Dove of peace

McGovern campaign badge

President McGovern '72

PEACE CANDIDATE
The Democratic Party chose Senator George McGovern of South Dakota to run against President Nixon in 1972. McGovern was himself a decorated World War II bomber pilot and was highly regarded in Congress. Yet he could not unify Democrat voters behind his promises to end the war and cut defence spending. Nixon won a landslide victory.

US withdrawal begins

I<small>N</small> 1969, P<small>RESIDENT</small> N<small>IXON</small> <small>PRESSED</small> the military for the "Vietnamization" of the conflict. This meant improved training and arming of South Vietnam's military, which was to take a larger role in defending the country. It also involved the withdrawal of US forces, which numbered 543,000 by that spring – the largest amount of the war. ARVN soldiers had shown they could fight well if led by good commanders. Unfortunately, too many of their top officers – including President Nguyen Van Thieu, overall commander – lacked military ability. On the other hand, ARVN forces led by able officers showed steady improvement during 1969. Still, it would be years before the Americans could be completely replaced. Nixon hoped to limit US casualties, but bloody battles continued. Many US soldiers became angry with the Nixon administration for sending them into action while the military was gradually leaving Vietnam.

North Vietnamese flag

RVN flag

A VICTORY
South Vietnamese security forces fighting alongside the ARVN proudly show off a captured North Vietnamese flag. Communist flags and a cache of VC arms and munitions were taken during counter-insurgency operations near the DMZ.

CREIGHTON ABRAMS
General Abrams (1914–1974) took command of MACV in 1968, replacing General Westmoreland. Abrams was ordered to end large-scale US operations and supervise the "Vietnamization" of the war.

HOMEWARD BOUND
Troops of the 9th Infantry Division board a Chinook helicopter to begin their journey back to the United States. They were part of a 25,000-strong troop withdrawal that began in June 1969.

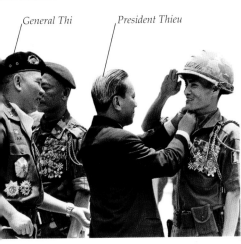

General Thi   President Thieu

CHEST FULL OF MEDALS
South Vietnamese president Thieu pins another medal on a well-decorated officer. Thieu is joined by General am Quang Thi (b. 1932), commander of the National Military Academy. Thieu was criticized for making any bad military decisions. He and Thi led the effort o build up their forces during Vietnamization.

NGO QUANG TRUONG
General Truong (b. 1929) shows captured enemy weapons to visiting US secretary of state William P. Rogers. A top ARVN commander, Truong was highly regarded by US officers as well as by his own troops.

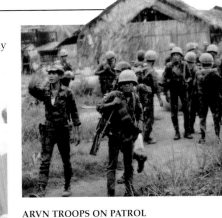

ARVN TROOPS ON PATROL
South Vietnamese Marines gather at a village in the Mekong Delta on a mission to cut a VC supply route. As US troops were withdrawing, ARVN forces assumed more patrol and reconnaissance duties. The best South Vietnamese troops proved themselves to be effective soldiers. To build a larger military, the government began drafting men between the ages of 17 and 43.

Hamburger Hill

On 10 May 1969, heliborne troopers of the 101st Airborne assaulted NVA forces dug in on top of Ap Bia Mountain, near the Laotian border. The military labelled this peak Hill 937. A savage battle raged for 10 days, costing 46 American deaths and 400 wounded. Troopers named he mountain "Hamburger Hill", because they felt they had been hrown into a meat grinder. Joined by ARVN troops, they captured Ap Bia but soon were ordered to abandon it. Many Americans, specially soldiers, believed the losses had been for nothing. Nixon now ordered General Abrams to avoid further engagements that would esult in heavy US casualties. Hamburger Hill was the last major battle ought by American troops in the Vietnam War.

Dragon

Leopard

Yellow
Leopard patch

Black
Dragon patch

ARVN PATCHES
These shoulder patches were worn by hard-hitting South Vietnamese Special Forces units. The Black Dragons attacked the Ho Chi Minh Trail in Laos and Cambodia. The Yellow Leopards were daring paratroopers.

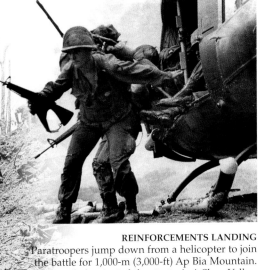

REINFORCEMENTS LANDING
Paratroopers jump down from a helicopter to join the battle for 1,000-m (3,000-ft) Ap Bia Mountain. The peak dominated the strategic A Shau Valley, where NVA forces operated in large numbers. This valley was a route for Communist troops and supplies to penetrate the Central Highlands region.

MEDICS AID THE WOUNDED
American and ARVN "walking wounded" make their way down Ap Bia Mountain with the help of medics. The 10-day fight for "Hamburger Hill" has just ended after the capture of the last NVA positions. These soldiers pass other wounded, who soon will be taken to a rear area for treatment. Many will fly out by medevac helicopters, but those only slightly injured will return to their units.

Last air assaults

DURING 1970, US FORCES steadily withdrew, but US air power continued to support the South Vietnamese. President Nixon ordered bombing raids against Communist positions in Cambodia, which further angered antiwar activists at home. Brief incursions (invasions) by US and ARVN forces struck Communist bases in Cambodia. Early in 1971, ARVN troops entered Laos, but were routed with severe losses. By 1972, there were no more American offensive operations. Only 70,000 US troops remained in Vietnam. In February, President Nixon visited China and opened diplomatic relations with Premier Zhou En-lai's government. That March, General Giap sent 125,000 troops on the attack, backed by tanks and artillery. ARVN units fell back until a heavy US bombing campaign blunted the invasion. Code-named "Linebacker", the air campaign also struck strategic targets in North Vietnam. Then the ARVN counterattacked, pushing back the Communists. Giap's bold assault, known as the Spring – or Easter – Offensive, was soundly defeated.

NIXON AND ZHOU TOAST
When Nixon visited Beijing, Vietnamese Communists worried he would make a deal to withdraw Chinese support from Hanoi. They opposed any call for peace that would leave Vietnam divided.

Map labels
NORTH VIETNAM
CHINA
NVA bases and supply routes
DMZ
Quang Tri
Hué
LAOS
Kontum
Pleiku
CAMBODIA
SOUTH VIETNAM
Central Highlands
An Loc
Tay Ninh
Saigon
Mekong River
South China Sea
N W E S

✻ Battle sites
Areas lost by S. Vietnam in 1972
NVA Eastertide Offensive

KEY BATTLES OF 1972
Giap's 30 March offensive surprised ARVN defenders, who fought hard as they fell back. The invasion brought on major struggles at Kontum, Quang Tri, and An Loc. The Communists were defeated by September.

ADVANCING NVA SOLDIERS
Camouflaged NVA troops trudge along a trail in Cambodia, heading for South Vietnam. They are on the way to join the Spring Offensive of early 1972.

AWAITING A LIFT
South Vietnamese airborne troops near the town of An Loc in April 1972 prepare for helicopter transport. An Loc was between the Communists and their objective – the capital city of Saigon, about 120 km (75 miles) away.

PREPARING TO FIRE
An NVA soldier loads a shell into a mortar – one of the main Communist weapons. Most mortars could be carried into action by two soldiers, while other troops brought up the ammunition.

JAMES F. HOLLINGSWORTH
General Hollingsworth (b. 1918) planned the air attacks that helped defeat NVA assaults at An Loc. Hollingsworth was serving as the senior military advisor to the ARVN corps defending Saigon.

Wright brothers' plane

AIRCRAFT CARRIER CREWMAN PATCH
The USS *Kitty Hawk* was one of the Navy carriers whose jets helped stem the Communist Spring Offensive. The carrier was named in honour of the North Carolina site where the Wright brothers first flew.

230-kg bomb

LOADING BOMBS
Navy crewmen on the carrier USS *Constellation* load fighter-bombers with 230-kg (500-lb) bombs for the Linebacker campaign. This carrier was one of five Navy "flattops" stationed off Vietnam. The air campaign also dropped mines into North Vietnamese harbours. These mines threatened commercial shipping carrying supplies for Hanoi's war effort. Linebacker would be followed by a second bombing campaign known as Linebacker II (see pages 56–57).

Shark-tooth decoration

Cobra helicopter crewman's patch

Rockets

COBRA HELICOPTER
Cobra attack helicopters such as this Air Cav gunship were among the best weapons employed in the Linebacker air campaign. The rocket-armed Cobra was an especially effective tank-destroyer during the Spring Offensive of 1972. More than 200 Soviet-made tanks led the offensive, but they were no match for Cobras. By mid-May, Cobras firing antitank rockets had blunted a major armoured offensive at Kontum in central Vietnam.

ARVN COUNTERATTACK
Tanks of a South Vietnamese armoured unit penetrate NVA lines during the ARVN counterthrust at Quang Tri. The Communists could not overcome US command of the air, so ARVN tank crews did not worry about attacks from above. South Vietnamese forces in this sector were led by General Ngo Quang Truong, who proved to be the most able ARVN general. Truong recaptured Quang Tri Province in a grinding campaign that lasted throughout September.

ANTITANK WEAPON
The shoulder-fired LAW (light antitank weapon) was crucial in the ARVN's battle with NVA tanks. The LAW launched 66-mm rockets that could knock out Soviet-made armour.

AIR FORCE PATCH
The 1972 build-up of US heavy bombers in the Pacific was code-named "Operation Bullet Shot". More than 12,000 personnel and 150 B-52s were readied at Andersen Air Force Base in Guam. From Guam, the high-altitude B-52s flew approximately 4,800 km (3,000 miles) each way to attack North Vietnam.

The Christmas Bombing

As the 1972 Communist offensive continued, peace talks were under way in Paris. Henry Kissinger (b. 1923) – a close advisor to Nixon – was head of the American delegation. In October, Kissinger announced an agreement was at hand, and Nixon called off the air campaign. Then it turned out that the Vietnamese Communists refused the US condition that Vietnam remain divided. When the talks broke down, Nixon decided to bomb North Vietnam into accepting a cease-fire agreement. He launched Linebacker II, bombarding North Vietnam from 18–30 December. Termed the "Christmas Bombing", this was the heaviest bombing of the war. It ruined the nation's industrial capacity and transport system and forced the Communists to accept a cease-fire.

HEROISM MEDAL
The Distinguished Flying Cross (DFC) is awarded for heroism in flight, both in combat or noncombat. Two DFCs were awarded during the Linebacker II campaign.

Identification number

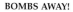

BOMBS AWAY!
A "string" of 340-kg (750-lb) bombs falls from a B-52D Stratofortress over Vietnam. Air Force and Navy warplanes pounded the cities of Hanoi and Haiphong with 18,000 tonnes of bombs. The bombing was so massive that the warplanes soon found few remaining targets worth attacking.

Weaving leaves and brush together

70162

B-52 WING PATCH
The 449th Bombardment Wing flew B-52s over Southeast Asia. They also flew KC-135 tanker aircraft, which provided mid-air refuelling services.

Black underside for camouflage in night bombing

ANTIAIRCRAFT DEFENCES
North Vietnamese militia load an antiaircraft gun in December 1972. US fixed-wing aircraft losses numbered 26 during Linebacker II – 15 of these were B-52s. Antiaircraft artillery and MiG fighters shot down three planes each, SAMs downed 17, and three crashed for unknown reasons. By the campaign's end, the North's air defences had run out of ammunition or had been destroyed.

US AIRCRAFT DOWN
North Vietnamese women salvage parts from the wreckag of an F-111 fighter-bomber. The Air Force lost two such aircraft in Linebacker II. Of the 26 planes lost, 20 were Air Force (which also lost a helicopter) and 6 were Navy

Palm leaves

CONCEALING A BRIDGE

North Vietnamese villagers camouflage a bridge with brush and leaves. This made it difficult for US warplanes to discover from above. Air attacks targeted bridges to cut transport links. Camouflage protected the small bridges that were essential to the movement of the people. Large bridges, however, were easy targets for US bombers. The Vietnamese had fought for years against enemies who had control of the air.

Camouflage

Clearing wood debris

LE DUAN (1907–1986)

Younger leaders such as Le Duan gained power with the death in 1969 of Ho Chi Minh. A high official in the Communist Party, Le Duan pushed for Vietnam's reunification. He favoured military action over any agreement that left Vietnam divided. Le Duan was willing to let the peace talks collapse if unsatisfactory terms were offered.

HOSPITAL IN RUINS

Doctors and nurses pick their way through the rubble of a Hanoi hospital destroyed by the Christmas Bombing. They are looking for supplies that can be saved. US airmen tried to avoid damaging hospitals and schools, but high-altitude bombing was not accurate enough to prevent such destruction.

Paris Peace Accords

As US air raids hammered North Vietnam in December 1972, Communist delegates to the Paris peace talks agreed to a cease-fire. On 27 January 1973, the Paris Peace Accords were signed by the United States, North Vietnam, South Vietnam, and the Viet Cong. The accords provided for a cease-fire, with the United States withdrawing from Vietnam. Vietnamese troops in the field would hold their present positions while their leaders consulted on the future. North Vietnam's top delegate, Le Duc Tho (1910–1990), and Kissinger were awarded the Nobel Prize for Peace in 1973. Tho declined to accept, however, saying the accords did not guarantee a lasting peace. He proved right, as large-scale warfare began again in 1975.

Round conference table

DISCUSSING PEACE TERMS

Paris peace talks delegates gather at a round table, so no country could claim the "head of the table" and be symbolically in charge. A cease-fire was accepted on 27 January 1973. Secretary of State William P. Rogers signed for the United States.

Le Duc Tho

DELEGATES IN PARIS

Henry Kissinger, left, converses with North Vietnam's Le Duc Tho through an interpreter, centre. These diplomats were heads of their delegations to the peace talks. They first began secret negotiations in 1970. Kissinger developed Nixon's Vietnamization policy of withdrawing US troops from Vietnam. Le Duc Tho was determined to reunify Vietnam, even at high cost to his people.

MADAME BINH

Madame Nguyen Thi Binh (b. 1927) signs the cease-fire agreement in Paris for the National Liberation Front and Viet Cong. Madame Binh was one of the most important NLF leaders. Throughout the Paris negotiations, the dignified Madame Binh was often seen on US television as the public face of the NLF.

Prisoners of war

MORE THAN 660 US SERVICEMEN were taken prisoners of war (POWs). A few were held as long as nine years, and some escaped. Approximately 470 were held in North Vietnam – many were abused, others tortured. Another 260 were in jungle detention camps in South Vietnam, Laos, and Cambodia. Thousands of Communists were captured, but the ARVN routinely killed captives instead of imprisoning them. The Paris peace negotiators agreed to release all POWs when the American military left Vietnam. In early 1973, Operation Homecoming airlifted former US POWs back to the United States. By March, 591 POWs had returned. Nixon soon assured the nation that everyone was freed, but some 2,400 men missing in action (MIA) still remain unaccounted for.

POW/MIA FLAG
The National League of POW/MIA Families designed this flag to remember Vietnam War prisoners and the missing. It is the only flag other than the Stars and Stripes to be displayed in the Capitol Rotunda in Washington, DC, or to fly over the White House.

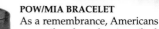

POW/MIA BRACELET
As a remembrance, Americans wore silver bracelets inscribed with the names of POWs or MIAs and the dates of their capture or disappearance.

A NURSE'S COMFORT
For three months, Navy nurse Lt Patricia Anderson wore a bracelet bearing the name of Lt Charles Norris. When he was released, she helped nurse him back to health.

Nurse Patricia Anderson

PARADE OF PRISONERS
American POWs are marched under military guard through the streets of Hanoi in 1966. They were filmed for propaganda purposes, and their images broadcast around the world. American POWs were mostly Air Force and Navy flyers, captured when their planes were shot down. During the war, 30 American POWs managed to escape.

FIRST TASTE OF FREEDOM
American POWs under North Vietnamese guard disembark from a bus on their way to a Hanoi airport in early 1973. They will take a flight to freedom, with their first stop in the Philippines. The release was arranged at the Paris peace talks. Operation Homecoming transported hundreds of former POWs back to the United States, where they were awarded special POW medals.

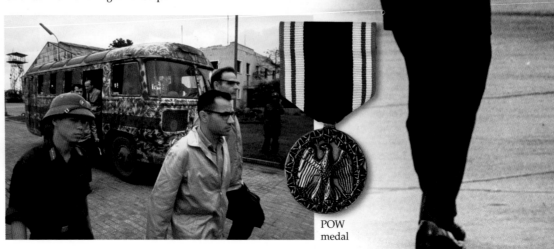

POW medal

Communist POWs

There is no accurate estimate of the thousands of Communist fighters and sympathizers imprisoned during the war. NVA and VC captives were sent to POW camps in South Vietnam. On the way, they were usually interrogated, often brutally – especially if taken by the ARVN. In camp, they were classified by rank, assigned serial numbers, fingerprinted, and photographed. Also, they were issued clothing, toilet articles, and mess gear. The terms of the Paris Peace Accords arranged for an exchange of prisoners between the Communists and the United States.

Communist star

Hands breaking free from chains

NVA POW medal

POW medal

Victory medal

FORMER NVA POW
The Communists honoured their own former POWs, as seen in this photograph of Nguyen Huu Thanh. Once an American captive, Thanh wears the NVA's POW medal pinned to his shirt pocket.

⌐REARY ACCOMMODATIONS
⌐merican POWs are seen at the ⌐Ianoi Hilton", as they nicknamed ⌐eir prison. One prisoner has been ⌐rmitted to talk with others who ⌐e locked in their cells.

A JOYFUL WELCOME
Returning Air Force colonel Robert L. Stirm hurries to the arms of his family as they greet him at Travis Air Force Base in California in March 1973. Stirm had been a prisoner of war for more than five years.

A SURVIVOR AND CAPTIVE
A soldier of the NVA 304th Division sits, bound and battle-shocked, under the watchful eye of a trooper from the 1st Air Cavalry Division. The prisoner was taken during fighting in the Ia Drang Valley of the Central Highlands, which saw heavy NVA losses.

Binding rope

TAKING IN SUSPECTS
A US officer, pistol in hand, pushes along suspected members of the Viet Cong being brought in for interrogation. The prisoners are bound with a rope to keep them from trying to run away. The youthfulness of the captives is typical of many South Vietnamese who seemed to be farmers but were actually guerrillas.

The fall of Saigon

IN 1973, THE UNITED STATES promised to strike back at the Communists if they resumed attacking South Vietnam. This promise was not kept. That same year, Congress cut off funds for US military involvement in Southeast Asia. Later, Congress cut military aid to the Saigon government. When the NVA invaded the RVN province of Phuoc Long in December 1974, President Gerald Ford could do nothing in response. The Communist offensive had begun. The South Vietnamese knew they had been abandoned by America – their morale was crushed. The NVA's final campaign went into full swing in March 1975. Now, the NVA were better armed than the ARVN. In a lightning war, the NVA swept through South Vietnam, capturing Saigon in April. This campaign ended almost 30 years of continuous fighting in Vietnam.

GERALD R. FORD (b. 1913)
In August 1974, Vice President Ford replaced Nixon, who had resigned after a political scandal. Although the NVA offensive violated the 1973 accords, Ford's administration did not fight it. Congress – and most Americans – were weary of the Vietnam War, so the United States refused to defend South Vietnam.

VAN TIEN DUNG (1917–2002)
General Dung had been the NVA commander in chief since 1953 and fought at Dien Bien Phu. In 1975, personally led the final campaign that broke through ARVN defences in the Central Highlands and charged on to Saigon.

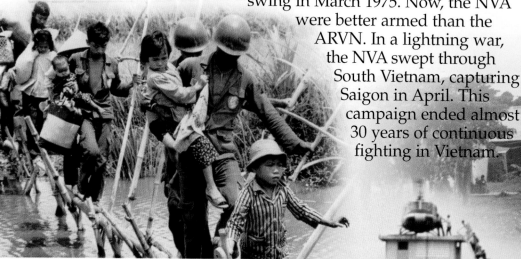

LOOKING FOR A SAFE PLACE
ARVN soldiers help fleeing villagers cross a bamboo footbridge over an irrigation ditch. NVA and VC forces are approaching this area, 80 km (50 miles) northwest of Saigon. Hordes of frightened South Vietnamese left their homes to escape the fighting. Many ran out of food and water and had no shelter; thousands died along the way. Many soldiers left their military units to rejoin their families attempting to get away from the invading Communists.

THE STRUGGLE TO ESCAPE
Frightened Saigon residents wave identification documents as they try to board a US Embassy bus on 24 April 1975. They are desperate for transport to the airport and hope to be flown out of the country. Those who worked for the government or the Americans were in danger of punishment by NVA forces surrounding the city.

LAST-MINUTE EVACUATION
A US helicopter loads passengers from a rooftop helipad near the US Embassy on 29 April. By the end of the next day, helicopters had evacuated more than 3,000 Americans, South Vietnamese, and other foreign nationals from the embassy compound. On that day, South Vietnam's government surrendered. Another 400 people trying to escape Saigon were left behind at the embassy as Communist forces entered the city.

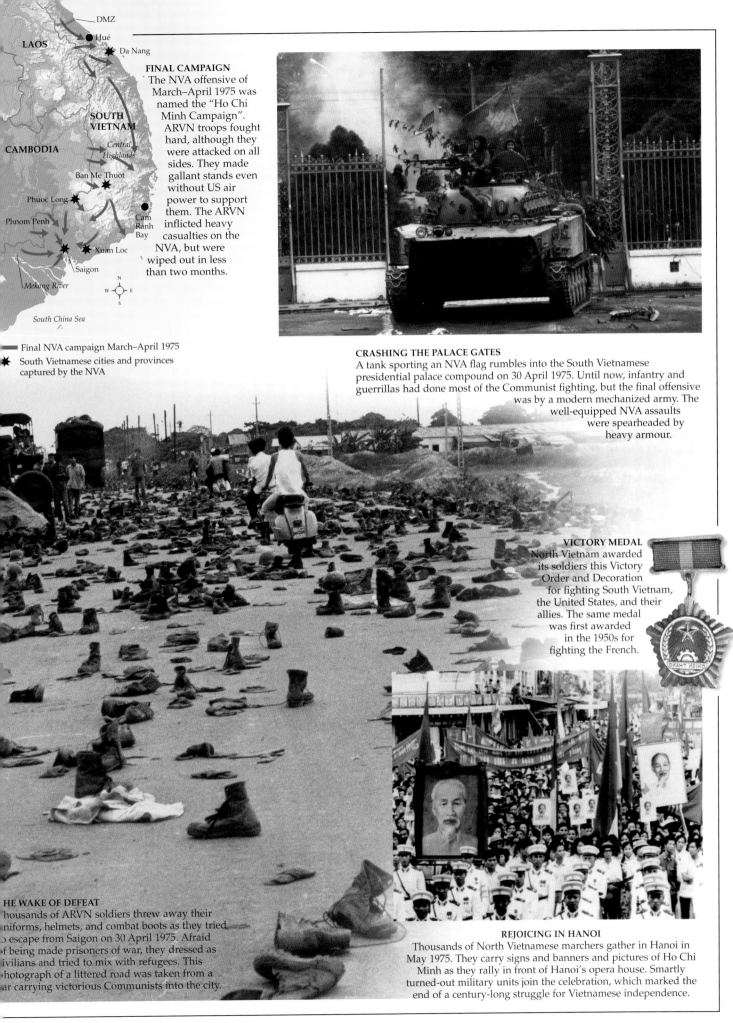

FINAL CAMPAIGN
The NVA offensive of March–April 1975 was named the "Ho Chi Minh Campaign". ARVN troops fought hard, although they were attacked on all sides. They made gallant stands even without US air power to support them. The ARVN inflicted heavy casualties on the NVA, but were wiped out in less than two months.

Final NVA campaign March–April 1975

South Vietnamese cities and provinces captured by the NVA

CRASHING THE PALACE GATES
A tank sporting an NVA flag rumbles into the South Vietnamese presidential palace compound on 30 April 1975. Until now, infantry and guerrillas had done most of the Communist fighting, but the final offensive was by a modern mechanized army. The well-equipped NVA assaults were spearheaded by heavy armour.

VICTORY MEDAL
North Vietnam awarded its soldiers this Victory Order and Decoration for fighting South Vietnam, the United States, and their allies. The same medal was first awarded in the 1950s for fighting the French.

THE WAKE OF DEFEAT
Thousands of ARVN soldiers threw away their uniforms, helmets, and combat boots as they tried to escape from Saigon on 30 April 1975. Afraid of being made prisoners of war, they dressed as civilians and tried to mix with refugees. This photograph of a littered road was taken from a car carrying victorious Communists into the city.

REJOICING IN HANOI
Thousands of North Vietnamese marchers gather in Hanoi in May 1975. They carry signs and banners and pictures of Ho Chi Minh as they rally in front of Hanoi's opera house. Smartly turned-out military units join the celebration, which marked the end of a century-long struggle for Vietnamese independence.

Aftermath

THE VIETNAM WAR COST the lives of more than 58,000 Americans, with more than 153,000 seriously wounded. One million Vietnamese combatants and 4 million civilians were killed. The number of Vietnamese wounded is unknown. The new Socialist Republic of Vietnam was a nation shattered by war, and bitterness remained between Communists and non-Communists. Hundreds of thousands of former RVN officials and officers were imprisoned. Many people tried to escape to other countries, especially to the United States. Most left in small, overcrowded boats. As Vietnam struggled to recover, its population grew from 49 million in 1976 to 82.6 million by 2004. Three-quarters of the people live in rural areas, and most work in agriculture. Vietnam is modernizing, but it lags behind other, more progressive Asian nations.

NATIONALIST POSTER
Hanoi became Vietnam's capital, and Saigon was renamed Ho Chi Minh City – where this poster was seen in 1980. It shows the dove of peace over a united Vietnam guarded by a soldier.

IN A MONASTERY
This Buddhist monk is a former ARVN soldier who devoted himself to a religious life. The Communist government restricts Buddhism and has taken over Buddhist hospitals, schools, and other institutions. Vietnam's Buddhists believe only faith and compassion can help heal their country.

REMEMBERING THE FALLEN
Visitors to a cemetery honour fallen NVA soldiers during the Vietnamese New Year in 1985. Burning incense sticks are placed beside graves as a way of honouring the dead. ARVN cemeteries, however, are usually neglected, and are considered the graves of enemies of the state.

MOTHERS' MEDAL
The sacrifices of North Vietnam's wartime mothers were recognized by this 1994 medal, accompanied by the title "Hero Mother".

A TIME OF PEACE
In 2003, young Vietnamese newlyweds pose before a statue of Ho Chi Minh, in Ho Chi Minh City. The statue was erected after the war. The former Saigon, population 7 million, is Vietnam's largest city.

The boat people

As Saigon fell, modern history's largest mass flight of refugees by sea began. Fearing the Communists, hundreds of thousands of South Vietnamese fled in small vessels. Termed "boat people", they made long, dangerous journeys to other countries in the region. Many drowned at sea. Some families spent their life savings to send their children off in a boat. They hoped their children would make a new start and help the rest of the family follow later. More than a million refugees from the conflict in Indochina eventually settled in the United States.

RESCUED
Fleeing the Communists, these South Vietnamese boat people have been rescued from a leaking vessel in the South China Sea. They are mainly former government officials or soldiers and their families. The next waves of boat people would be Vietnamese farmers and labourers seeking better economic conditions elsewhere.

IN HONG KONG HARBOUR
Vietnamese refugees huddle on an overcrowded boat in Hong Kong harbour in 1979. In this year, almost 69,000 boat people reached Hong Kong, making a 1,600-km (1,000-mile) journey. Boat people included many Amerasians – the children of Vietnamese women and US military personnel.

Overloaded vessel is dangerously low in water

Vietnam veterans

Allied forces' veterans often faced resentment when they returned home. Many people believed they had lost the war and had not been dedicated enough. Others believed they had fought in an unjust war. At first, some older veterans' groups in the United States did not want to accept Vietnam veterans as members. In time it became clear how well Allied servicemen and women had done their duty. Then Vietnam veterans were given the respect they had earned serving their country in extremely difficult conditions. Approximately 2.64 million US personnel served within the borders of South Vietnam from January 1960 to March 1973. Of this total, almost 1.6 million fought in combat, provided combat support, or were exposed to attack.

Fuse (or trigger)

LAND MINES
Thousands of land mines like this Soviet-made antitank mine remain uncleared in Vietnam. By 2004, approximately 40,000 Vietnamese had died and thousands more had been injured by land mines left after the fighting stopped.

VETERAN'S BUCKLE
This belt buckle commemorates Australian service in Vietnam.

WRITTEN IN STONE
An American Vietnam veteran touches "The Wall", a memorial bearing the names of US dead from the war. This national memorial in Washington, DC, was dedicated in 1981 (see pages 68–69).

LIFE GOES ON
A farmer's elephant lumbers by a rusting tank more than ten years after war's end. By 1985 this abandoned tank had not been removed from its resting place in Quang Tri Province. The modern war machine is useless, but the traditional beast of burden is still at work in Vietnam's countryside. Vietnam had an enormous task clearing away ruined military equipment after the conflict.

US VETERANS
Vietnam War veterans parade past saluting spectators during 1993 Veterans Day events at the national Vietnam Veterans Memorial in Washington, DC More than 8.2 million veterans served in the US military, around the world, during the Vietnam era. They accounted for more than one-third of all US veterans in 2004 and were the largest single group of living veterans from America's wars.

Did you know?

FASCINATING FACTS

One-third of the top National Liberation Front (NLF) political officers were women. Among the most important was Nguyen Thi Binh, chief representative of the NLF at the Paris peace talks. Many of these women entered the Vietnamese government after the war.

"Mining" warplanes for precious metals could be profitable. As much as $5,000 worth of gold, silver, and platinum could be found in the instruments and quipment of an American warplane.

US soldiers often painted an "Ace Of Death" playing card symbol on their vehicles. It was also carried by soldiers, who used it to frighten superstitious Vietnamese. The symbol was considered bad luck in Vietnam.

Death's Head playing card

US soldiers were supposed to destroy any letters they received. So, if a soldier were captured, the enemy would not be able to read his letters and find out personal information. Most troops kept their letters, however, and reread them often.

NVA officers in the field wore no distinguishing badge of rank. Instead, they carried pens to show they were officers. The pen was often secured with a short string and a safety pin and kept in a shirt pocket.

North Vietnamese officer's pen

In the early 1970s, the ARVN captured so many AK-47 assault rifles from the NVA that they gave away thousands to other Southeast Asian armies.

Documents that secretly circulated among Communist commanders and officials in South Vietnam were often stamped with symbols known only to those handling the papers.

An estimated 50,000 Vietnamese children were fathered by American servicemen during the Vietnam War. The men returned home, leaving mothers and children behind. These "Amerasian" children were discriminated against by the Vietnamese government, which considered them legally Americans. Some were taken to the United States for adoption, but most remained social outcasts in Vietnam.

The $8.4 million collected to erect the Vietnam Veterans Memorial in Washington, DC, included small contributions from more than 275,000 individuals.

The French author Bernard B. Fall was the leading authority on the Indochina conflict. US commander William C. Westmoreland studied Fall's works closely. A former French soldier, Fall attended college in the United States, where he became a college professor at Howard University in Washington, DC. His works, such as *Street Without Joy*, chronicled the First Indochina War. Fall was killed by a land mine in Vietnam in 1967.

NVA stamp for official documents

Soldiers on patrol were told not to use anything with a fragrance, such as soap, cologne, or shampoo. VC might detect these odours in the jungle and know US troops were nearby.

Of the 7,484 US women who served in Vietnam, 6,250 – or 83.5 percent – were nurses. Ten women serving in the military died, as did 56 civilians – including missionaries, nurses, and journalists. In a single tragedy, 37 of these civilian women died in a plane crash while escorting Vietnamese Amerasian orphans being flown out of the country in April 1975.

Just as US troops were entertained by well-known performers, the NVA and VC troops had their own entertainers. Performances were sometimes given in specially built underground theatre spaces in tunnels.

These girls, seen in Ho Chi Minh City, have Vietnamese mothers and American fathers.

Communist performers entertain North Vietnamese troops.

Montagnards sometimes gave US soldiers friendship bracelets and flutes.

Q Were any Vietnamese ethnic groups US allies?

A Yes, the Montagnards, or "mountaineers", were traditionally hostile to lowland Vietnamese, both Communist and non-Communist. The Hmong mountain people aided the Americans and became refugees after the war. Many built new lives in the United States.

Q What is a flash grenade and how is it used by the military?

A This device is like a hand grenade, but is non-lethal. The grenade's deafening bang and bright flash briefly confuse enemy troops, who then could be captured.

Q What nation has traditionally been Vietnam's worst oppressor?

A China: for 2,000 years, the Vietnamese struggled against Chinese rule. Their first rebellion was in AD39, led by the legendary Truong sisters. The Chinese were driven out but reconquered Vietnam a few years later. Vietnam gained freedom again in AD939.

Q Were the Vietnamese known historically as a warlike people?

A The Vietnamese battled five Chinese invasions after AD939, becoming excellent warriors. They defeated the mighty conqueror Kublai Khan three times – the last in 1287, routing 300,000 Mongol invaders. China finally recognized Vietnam's independence in 1427.

Q Ever hear of a "flying banana"?

A This was the nickname given to a series of large military transport helicopters that were banana-shaped. The powerful H-21 Shawnee has rotors "in tandem" – one at the front and a smaller rotor at the back.

Q Was the US K-9 Corps important in the war?

A Yes, the K-9 (for "canine", meaning "dog") Corps is the unit that trains dogs for various military duties. US troops used Alsatians as sentry dogs and to sniff out booby traps or find the disturbed soil of hidden VC tunnels. Scout dogs were so valuable that enemy mortars specifically targeted dog shelters for destruction.

Q What was the "domino theory"?

A This theory said that if South Vietnam fell to the Communists, then other Southeast Asian nations would fall – just as a row of dominoes standing on end can knock each other down.

Q When is the worst weather in Vietnam?

A Monsoon season has endless rain. There are summer and winter monsoons, depending on the region. Soldiers' clothing never dried, causing boils, disease, and infection from parasites.

Flash grenade

Q How educated were US soldiers in Vietnam?

A The average education of lower ranks (non-officers) in Vietnam was to first-year university level. Of those who volunteered, 79 per cent had high school diplomas (the equivalent of A-Levels).

Q Where did Americans meet the fiercest fighting?

A The north, where South Vietnam bordered both North Vietnam and Laos. Fifty-three per cent of Americans killed in Vietnam died in the four northernmost provinces: Quang Tri, Thua Thien, Quang Nam, and Quan Tin.

Q What was the prime air force target in North Vietnam?

A The 2.3-km (1.5-mile) Doumer Bridge, which carried the trains of four major railway lines coming from the north into Hanoi. All freight moving by rail from China and from the seaport city of Haiphong crossed this important bridge, which also carried lorry traffic.

K-9 unit soldier

Q Did South Vietnam's Buddhists demonstrate during the war?

A Yes, Buddhist monks regularly called for negotiations with the Communists. Priests praying in the streets for peace suffered oppression by government troops.

South Vietnamese Buddhist monks are penned in by barbed wire as they demonstrate in the early 1970s.

Timeline

In 1946, Vietnamese Communists and nationalists in eastern Indochina rose up against their French colonizers. This First Indochina War (1946–1954) ended with the defeat of the American-backed French. Vietnam was divided into the Communist North and capitalist South. For 20 more years, the United States supported South Vietnam, waging war against the Communists and nationalists. This Second Indochina War, known in the United States as the Vietnam War, cost the lives of more than 58,000 Americans, 1 million Vietnamese combatants, and 4 million Vietnamese civilians. In 1973, American troops withdrew from South Vietnam, which fell to the Communists two years later.

Destroyer USS *Maddox* in Gulf of Tonkin

1945–1946 INDOCHINA STRUGGLE
In August 1945, Japan surrenders to Allies in World War II (1939–1945) and gives up military control of French colonies in Indochina. Vietnamese Communist leader Ho Chi Minh declares the ndependent Democratic Republic of Vietnam (DRV). France sends troops to occupy Vietnam, sparking conflict; First Indochina War begins.

1950–1953 START OF US ADVISORY PHASE
US Military Assistance and Advisory Group (MAAG) is set up in 1950 to aid French against Vietminh, the rebel army. The United States supplies funding and military equipment to French forces. The insurgency strengthens and wins control of the countryside.

1954 TWO VIETNAMS
The fall in May 1954 of Dien Bien Phu, a major French base in northern Indochina, decisively ends the First Indochina War. Peace terms signed in Geneva, Switzerland, temporarily divide the country into the Vietminh-controlled DRV in the North and the Republic of Vietnam (RVN) in the South. Terms require that Vietnamese should vote on their form of government.

North Vietnamese stamp showing divided Vietnam

1955–1963 ARMED REVOLT
In 1955, Ngo Dinh Diem becomes president of South Vietnam. Backed by the United States, Diem refuses to allow a vote. Armed insurrection resumes, with the DRV supporting rebels known as Viet Cong (VC). US military advisors increase to 16,000 by 1963, when the Army of the Republic of Vietnam (ARVN) is defeated at Ap Bac.

1963 ASSASSINATIONS
On 2 November, an American-backed military coup in South Vietnam overthrows and assassinates Diem. US president John F. Kennedy is assassinated on 22 November; he is succeeded by Vice President Lyndon B. Johnson.

1964 GULF OF TONKIN INCIDENT
In August, the US military alleges that North Vietnamese gunboats have attacked a US vessel in the Gulf of Tonkin. The Senate passes Gulf of Tonkin Resolution giving Johnson broad war powers. Air strikes begin on North Vietnam.

1965 DIRECT US INTERVENTION
February–March VC attack US military base at Pleiku. In March, the first Marine combat troops are deployed to Vietnam, and the air campaign termed Operation Rolling Thunder begins. Johnson decides to increase US forces in Vietnam to 33,000 troops.

June–July Battle at Dong Xoai pits US Special Forces, sailors, and South Vietnamese troops against VC guerrillas. LBJ orders increase of US forces to 125,000.

Green beret

August Operation Starlite, first major US ground offensive; Operation Market Time attacks enemy seaborne supply routes to South Vietnam.

November Battle of Ia Drang Valley involves Air Cavalry assault, first major engagement by troops carried into battle and resupplied by helicopter. Pentagon calls for 400,000 troops.

1966 AIR AND GROUND WARFARE
January After a pause in bombing North Vietnam (in a failed attempt to begin negotiations) LBJ resumes air campaign.

March VC and North Vietnamese Army (NVA) troops attack and destroy US Special Forces base in A Shau Valley.

June Massive US air raids on Hanoi and the port city of Haiphong destroy much of North Vietnam's fuel supplies.

August Australian troops win Battle of Long Tan.

September–November Operation Attleboro drives VC forces across Cambodian border.

1967 WAR AND ANTIWAR
January Operation Bolo: air campaign inflicts heavy losses on North Vietnamese air force; in Operation Cedar Falls, US and ARVN troops attack the VC-controlled "Iron Triangle" region near Saigon.

February In Operation Junction City, US and ARVN strike enemy bases north of Saigon.

Peace-sign badge

April Major antiwar demonstrations in New York City and San Francisco indicate US public is not fully behind war.

Ngo Dinh Diem, front left, is welcomed at Washington National Airport by President Eisenhower, centre, 1957.

May Defence Secretary Robert McNamara decides war policy is not working; recommends cutting back on bombing. LBJ troubled by doubt over right course to follow.

July Marines battle NVA at Con Thien; McNamara visits Saigon, agrees to add 55,000 more troops.

August The US bombing campaign against North Vietnam intensifies.

October Huge antiwar march on Washington, DC; more than 50,000 protesters. Bombing of Hanoi/Haiphong increases.

November–December Battle of Dak To, a fierce clash between US and NVA. McNamara resigns, objecting to bombing.

1968 DEPTHS OF WAR
January–February Massive NVA-VC offensive during the Buddhist New Year, called Tet. South Vietnam is aflame for weeks before the US and government forces regain control.

January–April Siege of US base at Khe Sanh; Marines fight off determined NVA attacks and hold out until siege is broken.

President Johnson consults with Secretary of Defence Robert McNamara in February 1968.

March My Lai Massacre: US troops of the 23rd Infantry Division kill more than 300 civilians at the RVN hamlet of My Lai. Disheartened by growing opposition to the war, and his health failing, LBJ declares he will not run again for president.

July Phoenix programme begins: secret campaign to kill enemy sympathizers allegedly kills 40,000 South Vietnamese.

October LBJ announces end to bombing campaign Rolling Thunder. During Rolling Thunder, more bombs were dropped on North Vietnam than the United States used in the Pacific Theatre in World War II.

November Richard M. Nixon elected president, promising to bring peace with honour in Vietnam.

1969 PEACE DISCUSSIONS, WAR RAGES ON
January Preliminary meetings held in Paris for future peace talks. Marines conduct Operation Dewey Canyon, discovering network of enemy supply roads from Laos.

March Operation Menu: Nixon approves secret bombing campaign to strike enemy bases and supply routes in Cambodia. US begins policy of "Vietnamization", meaning South Vietnamese take responsibility for their own defence.

May 101st Airborne troops capture Hill 937 in the "Battle of Hamburger Hill," costing 46 US lives. Hill 937 is soon abandoned.

ARVN troops recapture Citadel at Hué, during Tet Offensive.

June Nixon announces that 25,000 troops will be withdrawn from Vietnam later in the year. Regular troop reductions will continue thereafter.

August US secretary of state Henry Kissinger meets with North Vietnamese representative in Paris.

September Ho Chi Minh dies in Hanoi at the age of 79.

1970 WIDENING WAR
April–May US troops invade Cambodia to attack Communist positions and bases.

May Ohio National Guard fires on antiwar demonstrators at Kent State University, killing four and wounding ten.

June Senate repeals Gulf of Tonkin Resolution that gave broad war powers to the president.

1971 VIETNAMIZATION AND WITHDRAWAL
February–April ARVN troops strike across Laotian border in Operation Lam Son.

November US troops number only 139,000, down from a peak of 543,500 on 30 April, 1969.

1972 BOMBS SPUR TALKS
February Nixon visits China, meets Mao Zedong and other leaders.

NVA attack in their 1972 offensive.

March–July NVA opens new offensives.

May–October In response to the NVA's offensives, Nixon orders Operation Linebacker, a massive bombing campaign against North Vietnam.

December Communist negotiators still hesitate to make peace, so Operation Linebacker II renews bombing, targets Hanoi and Haiphong.

1973–1975 COMMUNIST TRIUMPH
January 1973 Paris Peace Accords signed by US, North Vietnam, South Vietnam, and Viet Cong; US military presence in Vietnam ends 60 days later.

August 1974 Nixon resigns in disgrace after the Watergate scandal threatens to bring his impeachment. Vice President Gerald R. Ford takes office, pardoning Nixon for any illegal acts he had committed.

January 1975 North Vietnam resumes military campaign to defeat South Vietnam.

March–April 1975 Final Communist offensive captures Saigon on 30 April; North and South Vietnam are soon united as the Socialist Republic of Vietnam, with Hanoi as its capital.

US troops board a helicopter to return home in 1969.

Find out more

THE STORY OF THE INDOCHINA CONFLICT is found at many museums, libraries, and websites, and at war memorials. The memorials are places where everyone can join in remembering and honouring those who served. Major memorials are in the United States, Vietnam, Australia, South Korea, and France – some have interactive displays and guided tours that bring the wartime experience to life.

A national tribute

The Vietnam Veterans Memorial in Washington, DC, honours Americans who served in the Vietnam War. "The Wall" is the central feature, engraved with the names of those who died. Two other components, added later, are the Three Servicemen statue and flagpole, and the Vietnam Women's Memorial. The national memorial, which takes no stand for or against the war, is one of the most visited US monuments.

MEMORIAL IN AUSTRALIA
The Australian Vietnam Forces National Memorial, in the nation's capital, Canberra, was dedicated in October 1992. Its concrete forms are inspired by ancient sacred sites built of tall "standing stones". Soldiers' statements about the war are presented on an inside wall.

VIETNAM WOMEN'S MEMORIAL
This sculpture, by Glenna Goodacre, pays tribute to the women who served in Vietnam. Dedicated in November 1993, it shows three nurses with a wounded soldier. One nurse comforts him as another kneels in thought or prayer. The third nurse looks to the skies for help – perhaps from a medevac helicopter or from a higher power.

THREE SERVICEMEN
Fredrick Hart designed this memorial, which portrays soldiers in the field. It was dedicated in the autumn of 1984.

TAKING A RUBBING
Visitors to The Wall can place paper against an engraved name and rub with a pencil to create a copy. The National Park Service conducts ceremonies at the site on Memorial Day and Veterans Day.

THE WALL OF NAMES
A line of visitors forms under rainy skies at the Vietnam memorial in Washington, DC, in November 2004. This polished granite wall, designed by architect Maya Lin, holds the names of more than 58,200 US dead and missing. Dedicated in November 1982, the $8.4 million memorial was established by the Vietnam Veterans Memorial Fund, founded by Vietnam veterans.

Places to Visit

NATIONAL MUSEUM OF AMERICAN HISTORY, WASHINGTON, DC
Smithsonian's "The Price of Freedom: Americans At War" exhibit examines the ways war has shaped American history, and also features a display dedicated to the Vietnam War.

NATIONAL MUSEUM OF THE US AIR FORCE, DAYTON, OHIO
Visit the largest military aviation museum in the world. Featured are exhibits of US helicopters and fixed-wing aircraft of the Vietnam War.

NEW YORK VIETNAM VETERANS MEMORIAL, NEW YORK CITY
Excerpts of letters, diary entries, and poems written by Americans during the Vietnam era are etched into the New York Vietnam Veterans Memorial wall. These personal writings are supplemented by news dispatches and public statements.

VIETNAM-ERA EDUCATION CENTRE, NEW JERSEY VIETNAM VETERANS' MEMORIAL, HOLMDEL, NEW JERSEY
The first museum of its kind in the United States, the centre is dedicated solely to the Vietnam War. The collection includes photographs, historic timelines, films, interactive displays, personal letters, and more.

THE IMPERIAL CITADEL, HUÉ, VIETNAM
The Citadel, in Hué, was the residence of the Nguyen emperors. Hué was Vietnam's imperial capital from 1804 until 1945. Much of the Citadel was reduced to rubble during the Tet Offensive of 1968. The old fort and imperial structures are gradually being restored.

THE WEST POINT MUSEUM, WEST POINT, NEW YORK
The galleries of the West Point Museum interpret the history of the US Army from colonial times to the present. Weapons, uniforms, and art are featured in displays devoted to the Vietnam conflict. An NVA uniform is shown along with the muddy jungle fatigues of the American infantryman in Vietnam.

MEMORIAL IN FRANCE
The Memorial to the Wars in Indochina honours veterans of France's Indochina wars. Near Fréjus in southeastern France, the memorial was inaugurated in 1993. It holds the remains of more than 23,000 French – including 3,515 civilians – who died between 1940 and 1954. An educational room tells about France's century-long Indochina wars.

AUSTRALIA'S WAR MUSEUM
The Australian War Memorial is a museum that honours the dead from all the nation's wars. Located near Canberra, it is a place where loved ones can grieve. Also, the museum teaches understanding of war itself through exhibits and research facilities.

TUNNEL TOURS
The former VC tunnel complex at Cu Chi is one of Vietnam's most popular tourist attractions. The visitors' centre displays diagrams showing how the tunnels were used. Tours take visitors into the tunnels to see reconstructed living spaces, including barracks, meeting rooms, and kitchens.

USEFUL WEB SITES

- Comprehensive online research site, created in association with The Vietnam Project at Texas Tech University:
  star.vietnam.ttu.edu/index.htm
- Photographs from a North Vietnamese perspective:
  www.anothervietnam.com
- National Park Service site with an in-depth history of the making of the Vietnam Veterans Memorial:
  www.nps.gov/vive
- Visitors can use online technology to locate specific names and personal information of service members on The Wall:
  www.viewthewall.com
- An online museum of Vietnam War-era artifacts and other memorabilia:
  www.vietnamwall.org
- Great photographs and general information about the Vietnam War:
  www.vietnampix.com
- More about the Mobile Riverine Force, and war on Vietnam's waterways:
  www.mrfa.org

LEARNING ABOUT THE WAR
Vietnamese schoolchildren take a class trip to view a MiG-21 fighter at a Hanoi military museum in 2000. This plane was in the squadron that defended their city against US air raids. The trip is part of Vietnam's 25th-anniversary celebration of the 30 April 1975 fall of Saigon.

Glossary

AGENT ORANGE Toxic chemical used by American military to kill vegetation and thus deprive the enemy of food and hiding places in the jungle. Sprayed from aircraft and by hand. Many Vietnam veterans and Vietnamese suffer health problems caused by inhaling Agent Orange. Its name came from the orange stripe that identified its steel-drum containers.

AIRBORNE Soldiers who are trained parachutists, also called paratroopers. In Vietnam, these troops usually went into action on helicopters that carried them to battle.

AIR CAVALRY Nicknamed "Air Cav", these are helicopter-borne infantry who were supported by fire from helicopter gunships; many Air Cav troopers were members of former horse cavalry regiments.

AIRMOBILE Helicopter-borne (heliborne) infantry, such as Air Cav, whose units and tactics were first developed during the Vietnam War.

AK-47 assault rifle

AK-47 Soviet-manufactured Kalashnikov assault rifle that was a favoured weapon of the VC and NVA.

APC Armoured personnel carrier – an armour-plated vehicle used for transporting troops or supplies; usually armed with a .50-calibre heavy machine gun.

ARVIN Nickname for South Vietnamese soldiers in the Army of the Republic of (South) Vietnam.

ARVN Acronym for the Army of the Republic of (South) Vietnam: the South Vietnamese regular army.

BASE CAMP A central resupply base for units in the field; location for command headquarters, artillery batteries, and airfields.

BIRD Soldiers' term for a helicopter or any aircraft.

BOAT PEOPLE South Vietnamese refugees who fled by boat after the Communist victory in 1975. Boatloads of refugees sailed across the South China Sea, and many drowned. Those rescued were taken in by neighbouring countries and the United States.

BODY COUNT The military's count of the number of enemy troops that had been killed during an operation.

CHARLIE Nickname for Viet Cong or NVA; taken from "Victor Charlie", the military radioman's code for the letters *V* and *C* in messages about Viet Cong, or VC.

CHINOOK CH-47 cargo helicopter used to supply American and Allied troops.

CHOPPER A helicopter; Vietnam was the first "helicopter war" because it saw the first major use of rotary-wing aircraft for transporting troops during military campaigns.

CLAYMORE Widely used antipersonnel mine that, when detonated, hurled small projectiles up to 100 m (300 ft).

COBRA AH-1G attack helicopter, armed with rockets and machine guns.

COMPOUND A fortified US or Allied installation that served as a camp and fortress.

CONCERTINA WIRE Coiled barbed wire with razor-sharp edges that was laid to protect the outer perimeter of a fortified position. Enemy troops would have to cut this wire before they could break through and attack.

COUNTERINSURGENCY Organized antiguerrilla (anti-insurgent) warfare that armed and trained local militias to defend their communities against the enemy. Counterinsurgency methods included using guerrilla tactics of surprise, concealment, and assassination to strike at enemy guerrillas.

C-rations

C-RATIONS Combat rations, or meals, for use in the field; each meal usually included a canned main course and fruit, packets of dessert, powdered cocoa, sugar, cream, and coffee; there was also a packet of cigarettes and some chewing gum.

DEFOLIATION The process of destroying vegetation (foliage) usually by spraying toxic chemicals such as Agent Orange, widely used in Vietnam.

DMZ The Demilitarized Zone that was the dividing line between North and South Vietnam at the 17th parallel. The DMZ was established in 1954 under the Geneva Accords. It was to be kept free of any military installations or occupation.

DRV Democratic Republic of Vietnam – the original name given by Ho Chi Minh to Vietnam when he proclaimed independence from France in 1945. When Vietnam was divided in 1954, the name referred only to Communist-dominated North Vietnam, with the capital Hanoi.

Special Forces base camp in the Central Highlands

Dustoff buckle

DUSTOFF Emergency evacuation of the wounded by medical helicopter; a medevac.

FIRE BASE A temporary artillery encampment, or compound, set up to support nearby ground operations with cannon fire or rockets.

FIREFIGHT A brief battle, or exchange of small-arms fire, with the enemy.

FLAK JACKET A fibreglass-filled vest worn for protection from shrapnel – small pieces of metal hurled by the explosion of shells, mines, or grenades.

Flak jacket

FRIENDLY FIRE Accidental attacks on US or Allied soldiers by other US or Allied soldiers, aircraft, or artillery – usually the result of being mistaken for the enemy.

GREEN BERETS US Special Forces trained in counterinsurgency warfare and for operations behind enemy positions; they wore green berets.

GRUNT US infantry's humorous term for infantryman – the lowest in military status.

GUNSHIP An armed helicopter or fixed-wing aircraft used to support ground troops and to patrol in search of enemy activity.

HAMMER AND ANVIL Tactic of partially encircling an enemy position with one force while other units drive the enemy out of hiding. The first force is the anvil, and the second is the hammer that attempts to smash the enemy against that anvil.

HANOI HILTON Nickname of North Vietnam's Hoa Lo Prison given by Americans held prisoner there; Hiltons are famous luxury hotels found around the world.

HUEY Nickname for the UH-1 series of helicopters, which were used for many purposes during the war.

IN-COUNTRY A soldier serving in Vietnam was said to be "in-country".

IRON TRIANGLE Viet Cong-dominated area, mainly jungle and rice paddies, between the Thi Tinh and Saigon rivers northwest of Saigon.

LZ A landing zone, usually a small protected clearing near the battlefront for the landing of resupply helicopters. LZs often grew to become permanent base camps interrupting enemy supply lines or troop movements.

MAAG Military Assistance and Advisory Group; US headquarters formed in 1950 to aid the French military effort in Indochina.

MACV Military Assistance Command, Vietnam; headquarters that replaced MAAG in 1962; had overall command of US forces in Vietnam until 1973.

MEDEVAC Evacuation of the wounded from the battlefield by helicopter.

MIA "Missing in Action", the military term for a serviceman or woman whose whereabouts after combat is not known.

M-16 American assault rifle used by US and ARVN troops and many Allies.

NAM US and Allied soldiers' nickname for Vietnam.

NAPALM A jellied petroleum material which burns fiercely; fired from flamethrowers or contained in bombs that explode and spread flaming jelly.

NLF National Liberation Front, the political wing of the South Vietnamese insurgency fighting against the Republic of (South) Vietnam.

NVA North Vietnamese Army, the regular troops of the Democratic Republic of (North) Vietnam.

POW "Prisoner of War", a serviceman or woman who has been captured by the enemy; POWs have specific rights in accordance with the laws of war that have been accepted by most nations.

PUNJI STICKS Sharpened bamboo stakes set in camouflaged pits, or mantraps; punjis pierce the bodies of those who fall into the pit.

RANGERS Elite commandos in the US Army, specially trained for long-range reconnaissance (scouting) and dangerous combat missions.

RVN Republic of Vietnam, the official name given to South Vietnam when established in 1954 by its first president, Ngo Dinh Diem. The RVN capital was Saigon, the largest city in the South.

SEABEES Navy construction engineers famous for their ability to construct airfields, bases, and roads swiftly, often under combat conditions. Derived from the letters *CB* for "construction battalion".

SEALS Navy personnel who are members of special warfare "Sea, Air, Land" teams.

SEARCH AND DESTROY Operations in which troops searched an area in order to locate and destroy Communist forces; this often also included destroying supply caches and living quarters.

STRATEGIC HAMLETS Fortified villages, often in isolated farming areas, set up by US and ARVN forces to protect the people against attacks or threats from Communist insurgents. Local militia were trained to defend these compounds.

TET The Buddhist lunar New Year. Thousands of Viet Cong guerrillas attacked US and ARVN positions during the celebration of the Tet holiday in 1968.

TUNNEL RATS Originally termed "tunnel runners", the men who crawled into VC tunnels later took this nickname.

Tunnel-rat gas mask

VC Short for Viet Cong, which in turn is the Vietnamese nickname for South Vietnamese Communist guerrillas operating in South Vietnam.

VIETNAMESE POPULAR FORCES South Vietnamese local military units, usually militia forces made up of civilians rather than regular soldiers.

VIETNAMIZATION US policy to turn over the fighting to the South Vietnamese Army; this policy was established by President Richard M. Nixon late in the war, during the withdrawal of American troops.

ZIPPO A flamethrower that shot out flaming napalm; named after a type of cigarette lighter. A "Zippo" was also a gunboat armed with a flamethrower, and the phrase "Zippo job" referred to a mission to set Communist-held villages or positions on fire.

Zippo in a firefight

Index

Acknowledgments

DK Publishing, Inc. and Media Projects Inc., offer grateful thanks to: Clifford J. Rogers, Associate Professor of History, United States Military Academy; Steve R. Waddell, Associate Professor of History, United States Military Academy; Erika Rubel; Mark Tolf; David Mager; Michael Harris; Albert Moore; Doug Niven; Tim Page; Emma Naidoo; Jim Messinger; Bob Taylor; Justin Saffell; Ed Emering; Robert W. King; Ngo Vinh Long; Rev. Diedrik Nelson; Margie Ortiz and Terry Adams; Sema at Art-Hanoi; Ronnie Oldham; Jeff Lindsay; Tex Pantaleo; Robert H. Stoner, USNR (Ret.); Ron Toelke for cartography; Rob Stokes for relief mapping; Brian A. Benedict; Madeline Mancini; and Madeline Farbman.

Photography and Art Credits
(t=top; b=bottom; l=left; r=right; c=centre; a=above)
American Museum of Military History: 33bl.
joelscoins.com: 7tl. anothervietnam.com:
© Mai Nam, 21brc; © Tran Phac, 22tl; © Le Minh Truong, 22–23, 23cr, 25b, 40–41; © Vo Anh Khanh, 33br; © VNA, 44bl, 56–57tc; © Duong Thanh Phong, 46tl, 60–61. **Art-hanoi.com:** 4crt, 19bc.
Associated Press: 10bl, 13br, 38–39c, 69tl.
Australian War Memorial: 69tcl. **Bernie Boston:** 50bl. **Boston University Archives:** 39tr.
brownwater-navy.com: 42cr. **James Burmester:** 4clt, 15bc, 37br, 53cr. **Michael Burr:** 19r, 19bc.
Canadian Forces National Defense Ministry: 4crb, 63cl. **CORBIS:** 35cr, 58bl; © Alinari

Archives/CORBIS: 7tr; Bettman/CORBIS: 6cl; 7cr, 8tl, 8tr, 8–9, 9cl, 9bc, 10tr, 10c, 16bc, 17tc, 17br, 18b, 20br, 21br, 25tl, 31tc, 34bl; 34–35tc, 38tl, 38bl, 38bc, 39cl, 39crt, 40b, 42bl, 43tr, 43cr, 45br, 50cl, 50–51cl, 51tl, 51tr, 51cr, 51br, 53bl, 54–55, 55tr, 57tr, 57bl, 60bc, 60bl, 63tr; © George Hall/CORBIS: 34br; © Jeremy Horner/CORBIS: 62tl; © Hulton-Deutsch Collection/CORBIS: 21t; © John R. Jones, Papilio/CORBIS: 46cr, 69bcl; © Catherine Karnow/CORBIS: 64bl; © Wally McNamee/CORBIS: 63cr; © Francoise de Mulder/CORBIS: 61tr; © Tim Page/CORBIS: 38cl, 62-63b; © Steve Raymer/CORBIS: 63b; Reuters/CORBIS: 69bl; © Roman Soumar/CORBIS: 46br; CORBIS SYGMA: 6tr; © Darren Whiteside/Reuters/CORBIS: 57cr. **DK Picture Library:** © DK Picture Library: 48tl; © DK Picture Library, courtesy Museum of American Politcal Life/University of Hartford: 51br (inset); © Philip Blenkinsop/DK Picture Library: 70–71 bkgnd; © DK Picture Library, courtesy of Andrew L. Chernack: 23cl, 26b (scarf, canteen, pouch, oil can), 28cc (NVA knife); © David Mager/DK Picture Library, courtesy Mark Tolf: 2cr, 4tr, 4tc, 4bl, 11cl, 13cl, 15tr (inset), 27 lower cr, 27 upper c, 27tr, 29t (M-1 carbine, access.), 29cl (cleaning kit and grenades), 29c (M16 access.), 30bl, 30tl (inset), 30cl, 31tl, 31tr (inset), 32cl, 32bc, 33cl, 35tr (patches), 37bc, 38tr, 41c (inset), 47 (all equipment), 49bc, 51cr (inset), 55bl, 56cl (medal), 65bl, 66cr, 70tr, 71r; © Stephen Oliver/DK Picture Library: 11bc; © Tim Ridley/DK Picture Library, courtesy of

the Ministry of Defence Pattern Room, Nottingham: 2tcl, 28bcl (RPG-7 and accessories), 29tcr (M16A1), 29bcr (M79); © Laura Wickenden/DK Picture Library: 46bcl. **Emering Coll.:** 2tr, 9bl (inset), 14tr, 15c (inset), 20tl, 37tc, 37te, 37tcr, 37cr, 37b, 59tc (POW & medal), 61cr, 62cr. **Folio, Inc.** © Rob Crandall: 68cl. **Michael Harris:** 62cl. **Lyndon Baines Johnson Pres. Lib.:** 11br, 15t, 20tl, 24tl, 48cl, 67cl. **John F. Kennedy Pres. Lib.:** 11tr. **Robert W. King:** 21tr (inset). **Coll. Ted Laurenson/©Diggitt McLaughlin:** 4tl, 16tl, 17cl, 50tr, 66br. **LJMilitaria:** 20bc (inset), 55tc, 56tl, 56cl (patch). **John P. Conway/vhpamuseum.org:** 32tl, 55cr, 71tl. **Library of Congress:** 10–11cl, 11cr, 13tr, 14c, 14b, 16tr, 16bl, 16–17h, 17tl, 18cl, 19b, 21cl, 21bl, 23tc, 24b, 24cl, 26cl, 32cl, 39br, 45tc, 45cl, 45cr, 47tl, 47br, 49tr, 50tr, 52tr, 53cr, 53tl, 54cl, 55br, 57tc, 57br, 59tr, 60tl, 60cl (UPI), 61br, 66bc. © Jeff Lindsay: 65tl. **Mobile Riverine Forces Association/© Dan Dodd:** 34cl, 42c (two patches, inset), 42cr, 43tl, 71b. **MPI Archives:** 2c, 50t, 50c, 59br, 65b. **Andrea Morland:** 68tr. **National Archives:** 2br, 6bl, 8bl, 9tc, 12cl, 14tl, 14tcl, 15cr, 15bl, 16tc, 16tr, 16-17s, 17tr, 18tl, 19cl, 23tr, 23br, 24tr, 25tr, 25cr, 26-27c, 27tl, 27bl, 27ccr, 28tl, 28tr, 28br, 28cl (grenades), 29br, 32tr, 32bl, 33bc, 33tr, 35b, 36bl, 36-37, 37tl, 39tc, 40c, 41tr, 41cr, 41tr, 43tr, 44tr, 44cr, 44cl, 45tr, 46tcl, 46bl, 49cr, 52b, 53tl, 53tc, 54tr, 55c, 57cr, 57br, 60tr, 64-65 bkgnd, 65tr, 66-67 bkgnd, 67b, 70br. **NPS/Terry Allen:** 68b, 68-69 bkgnd. **National Vietnam War Museum:** 34c (inset). **Naval Hist. Soc.:** 12cr,

12–13cr. **Rev. Diedrik Nelson:** 4clb, 9r, 56cl.
Ronnie Max Oldham: 14cl. **Ngo Vinh Long:** 7cl, 23bc. **Stars and Stripes:** 39tl. **Texas Tech:** 25cl (inset), 29bl, 64tc, 64tr, 67tl, 70l; Anonymous Coll.: 58–59tc, 63tl, 64br; Peter Braestrup Coll.: 49br; Donald Jellema Coll.: 2tl, 28clt, 28bcr, 31cl, 31b, 56br, 64br, 67tr; Douglas Pike Coll.: 13tl, 15cl, 39cr (Cronkite), 48bl, 48cr, 54bl, 56bl; Brig. Gen. Edwin H. Simmons Coll.: 48-49bc. **Tim Page:** 1, 3, 15br, 30tl, 30-31, 31tr, 44-45b, 56bl, 56br, 62t. **Theodore Schweitzer III:** 58cl. **Tribune Media Service:** 38cr.
US Air Force: 20cl, 21tcr, 34tl, 36tl, 36tr. **US Army:** 17tr, 27crb, 49tl, 52cl, 55tl, 56-57cc. **US Army Ctr for Mil. Hist.:** 6-7bc, 11tl, 52tr (inset), 65tl. **US Army Mil. Inst.:** 65cr. **US Navy:** 12bl, 42tr, 43cl, 58bc (nurse). **US Navy, Naval Hist. Ctr:** 2 clb, 12c (inset), 12-13b, 66tr. **Vietnam Veterans Assoc. of Australia:** 4c. VietnamWall.org: 2bl, 2bc, 9tl (inset), 10cl, 25tl (patch), 26ct, 27br, 28bl, 30cr, 33cr, 58tl, 58tc (bracelet), 64tl, 65tl (bracelet & flute), 71cl.

Cover Credits:
Bettman/CORBIS: front b, back b; **DK Picture Library:** © DK Picture Library: front tl (sandal & helmet), front tr; © DK Picture Library, courtesy of Andrew L. Chernack: back tc, back c; © Tim Ridley/DK Picture Library, courtesy of the Ministry of Defence Pattern Room, Nottingham: back cl; **National Archives:** front (mine); **US Army Ctr. for Mil. Hist.:** front tc (flag), front tlc (medals); **VietnamWall.org:** back cr, back tl.

TRADITIONAL TALES

from

AFRICA

Vic Parker

Based on myths and legends retold by
Philip Ardagh

Illustrated by
Georgia Peters

Belitha Press

First published in the UK in 2001 by

Belitha Press Ltd
London House, Great Eastern Wharf,
Parkgate Road, London SW11 4NQ

ISBN 1 84138 173 X

British Library Cataloguing in Publication Data
for this book is available from the British Library.

Editor: Stephanie Turnbull
Designer: Zoë Quayle
Educational consultant: Margaret Bellwood

Printed in Hong Kong

960

960.

This book is due for return on or before the last date shown below.

CONTENTS

AFRICAN TALES

**Africa is an enormous place. It is not just one country,
it is a whole group of countries called a continent.
Africa makes up nearly a quarter of all the land on Earth.**

People have lived in Africa for thousands and thousands of years.
Because Africa is so huge, people from different parts of the continent
have their own languages, customs, religious beliefs and favourite
stories. These have spread all over the world, mainly because of the
slave trade. This was when white people took hundreds of Africans
to North America and the Caribbean islands and forced them to work
on farms. The Africans struggled for freedom for many years.

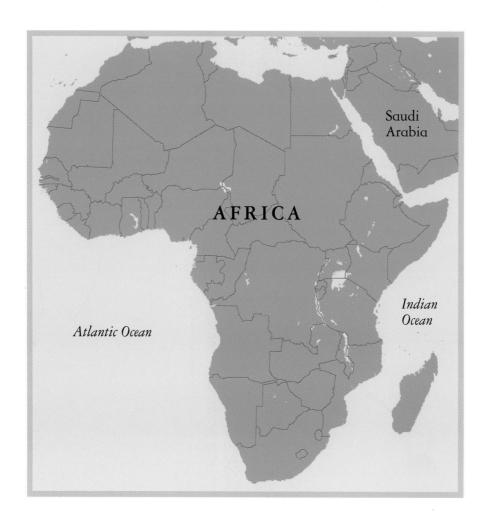

Much of Africa is covered by the world's largest desert, the Sahara. In other parts of Africa there is wide, thick jungle. Some African land is wild and difficult to farm. These areas are called the bush.

Over the years Africans have made up thousands of fantastic stories about the creatures who live in these places, such as the sly rats of the desert, the mischievous monkeys of the jungle and the lazy hippos of the plains. For hundreds of years, people have thought that gods and spirits lived in the bush, so there are many wonderful stories about them, too.

In this book you can read exciting new versions of these tales, taken from many different peoples and cultures within the huge continent of Africa.

This painted wooden mask was made in Nigeria. Masks are worn in special ceremonies to contact spirits.

IN THE BEGINNING

In the beginning, the creator god decided to make the world. He took a big lump of clay and moulded it into a smooth, round pot. He baked the pot in a huge oven, then he wrapped it in shining, red copper and set it in the sky. The creator god smiled.

'You are my Sun,' he said.

The creator god was so pleased with the Sun that he made another pot. This one was smaller and he wrapped it in pale brass. The creator put the gleaming pot at the other end of the sky, far away from the Sun.

'You are my Moon,' he said.

The creator god stood back and admired his work.

Hmmm, he thought. *The heavens are now very beautiful, but they need something else.*

He reached out and snapped off a bit of the Sun. He smashed it into a million pieces and scattered the fragments across the sky.

'Stars,' he announced. 'Perfect.'

Next the creator god shaped another giant lump of clay into a ball, which he called the Earth.

7

'You will be my wife,' he told the Earth and sent down the first ever shower of rain on it. To the creator god's joy, twins grew from the wet soil. He called his children Water and Light and they joined him in the heavens.

Water and Light saw that their mother Earth was naked and bare. They hurried to make grass and plants grow into a robe to cover her.

Meanwhile, the creator god shaped more clay into the first man and woman. He breathed life into them and set them on the Earth. The creator god was delighted when the woman gave birth to eight children.

'What interesting creatures these humans are!' smiled Light. 'Why don't you make some more?'

The creator god thought this was a good suggestion. He took some brilliant sunlight and made people with shining, black skins. He then took some gleaming moonlight and made people with pale, white skins.

'Well done!' said Water. 'They are all wonderful.'

The creator god sat and talked with Water and Light as they made a skirt of flowers and trees for their mother Earth. The plaiting and weaving of their hands created a breeze which blew their words far away.

Down on Earth, humans heard these strange sounds. They understood them and began speaking to each other.

Soon the humans realized that there were words for things they had never seen.

'We know the meaning of words such as *mountain* and *river*,' the people said to each other, 'but what are words such as *dog*, *giraffe*, *whale* and *parrot*?'

One clever woman worked it out.

'If these things aren't down here with us, they must live up in the heavens with the creator god,' she cried. 'He must want to keep them for himself!'

'Then we'll have to go up there and steal them!' whispered a man.

The humans built a hollow, wooden pyramid, big enough to contain all the things the creator god had kept for himself. They used a strong rope to drag the pyramid to the top of the highest mountain. A group of humans climbed up the pyramid, through the clouds and found themselves in the heavens.

The people could hardly believe the wonderful things they found there. All around were brightly-coloured furry things and feathered things and scaly things. Things were scampering and fluttering and swimming. Things were squeaking and squawking and snorting. The amazed humans finally understood the meaning of the words *animals*, *birds*, *fish* and *insects*.

'They're so beautiful!' the people cried. 'How clever the creator god is! We won't steal *all* his creatures. We'll just take one male and one female of each type.'

Quickly, the humans began to pack the pyramid with pairs of animals. The largest were wedged in at the bottom. The smallest were jammed in at the top. When the last creature had been squeezed inside and the huge doors bolted shut, the pyramid was far heavier than anyone had imagined. It was much too heavy to be lowered back down with the rope. There was only one other way to return to Earth – down the rainbow.

With their hearts beating fast, the people made sure that one end of the rope was tied tightly to the pyramid. They looped the other end round the Sun. Slowly, they began to lower the pyramid down the rainbow bridge...

Way below, the men and women who had been left on Earth caught sight of the giant pyramid sliding down the rainbow. They began to cheer, but suddenly the sky thundered with an ear-splitting CRACK! and their shouts of excitement turned to cries of terror. The pyramid was hurtling towards them and at the other end of the rope was a broken piece of the Sun! The people fled for cover as the burning fragment flew into a bush. It burst into a blaze of orange flames.

At first the people were terrified. They had never seen fire before, but once they recovered from the shock, they were very pleased.

'It is another gift from the creator god!' they yelled. 'It gives heat and light! Imagine what we can do with it!'

Finally, everyone rushed to open the doors of the pyramid. The animals, fish, birds and insects inside were unharmed. The humans gasped with joy as the creatures streamed out into their new home.

And that is how humans came to share the Earth with all sorts of animals. The creator god saw that his creatures were happy there, so he allowed them to stay.

THE RACE

The old king was very tired. Ruling was hard work and he had done it for many long years. The old king made up his mind – enough was enough. He deserved a rest. It was time to hand over his crown to one of his sons, Prince Lizard or Prince Frog.

But which one should be the new king? Prince Lizard was handsome and strong. He was also a fast mover and did everything quickly. Prince Frog was slower, but he was also more thoughtful. The king sighed and shook his head. He loved both sons equally and he couldn't decide between them. Also, he couldn't bear to upset one of them by not picking him. The old king shut his eyes and thought for a while...

That was it! The old king's eyes opened wide as a wise idea popped into his head. He wouldn't choose either of his sons – he would make them decide for themselves.

The old king called for his trusted chief minister and whispered his clever plan into the minister's ear. The chief minister nodded and smiled, then he hurried away to find the royal brothers.

The chief minister searched for a long time and eventually came across the two princes at a rocky pool. Prince Frog sat half-in and half-out of the water, under a shady leaf. He liked to be cool and damp. If he got too hot, it made him quite ill. Prince Lizard sat out in the open, in the full heat of the midday sun. His dry, scaly skin was baking nicely, just as he liked it. As usual, Lizard was boasting about what a good king he'd be one day. As usual, Frog was listening carefully and quietly.

'Good afternoon, your highnesses,' the chief minister greeted the princes. 'I come with an important message from his majesty, your father. He summons both of you to the palace immediately. Whoever gets there first, will be the next king.'

Prince Lizard cackled with delight. He knew that he was the speediest by far.

'Don't worry,' he teased his brother. 'If we've all gone to bed by the time you arrive, I'll tell them to keep the palace gates open for you.' With that he slithered away across the ground and slipped out of sight.

Prince Frog sat and watched him go.

'It's true,' he said to himself slowly and thoughtfully. 'My brother Lizard is much faster than I am. Besides, I can't go out in the blazing sun or I will shrivel up and die.'

Prince Frog shot out his tongue and swallowed a fly. 'I shall have to try some other way,' he decided.

Prince Frog hopped through the shady undergrowth until he reached a magic tree. Gently, he broke off a twig and ground it into powder. Carefully, he blew the powder into the wind. Loudly, he croaked some magic words. The skies suddenly grew darker, then... splosh! A large drop of rain landed on Prince Frog's nose. Splish! There was another, on the ground. Splash! Splash! Splash! The rain began to come thick and fast. Prince Frog looked up at the black clouds and grinned a wide grin. His spell had worked! Steadily, he hopped away through the puddles on his way to the palace.

Prince Lizard was very nearly at the palace when the downpour began. He hated getting wet and he hurried to take cover under a nearby rock.

It won't matter if I shelter here for a while, he thought to himself. *Frog will never catch up!*

He made himself comfortable and yawned. It was nice and dry under the rock and he was a little tired after all that running... In a few seconds, he was fast asleep.

When Prince Lizard woke, the drumming of the rain had stopped. He poked his nose out from under the rock and felt warm sunshine beating down.

'Splendid!' he said to himself. He shot out from under the rock and set off once again.

It wasn't long before Prince Lizard saw the magnificent royal palace in front of him.

'Just think!' he said to himself gleefully. 'Soon, all this will be mine!' Tears of pride came to his eyes as he heard the royal heralds trumpeting a fanfare to welcome him. Prince Lizard slowed to a dignified walk and the huge palace gates began to swing open to let him in.

Horror of horrors! It wasn't his father, the old king, who came out to greet him – but his brother! Prince Lizard's jaw dropped open.

'Prince Frog!' he squeaked. 'How... but... what... ' he began to stutter.

'Hello, Lizard,' said Frog. 'What kept you?'

Frog's magic rain shower had lasted long enough for him to catch up with Lizard – and to overtake him, too.

'By the way, I'm not *Prince* Frog now,' Frog continued, 'I'm *King*.' And there was nothing Lizard could do or say to argue with that!

So now you know that when you hear frogs croaking, you should take your umbrella out with you. They are saying the magic words that bring the rain...

KIGBO AND THE BUSH SPIRITS

Kigbo was the sort of person who always had to do things his own way. No one knew where he got his determined ideas from, as his parents were quiet, simple people. Perhaps it had something to do with his name, for 'Kigbo' means 'stubborn man'.

Eventually Kigbo got married and moved out of his parents' house. His father decided to make a suggestion to his stubborn son.

'Kigbo, it is time for you to stop working on my land,' he said. 'Now you have a wife to look after, you need a farm of your own. Why don't we clear some land at the edge of the village, so you can have your own field?'

But Kigbo had other ideas. 'That's little more than waste ground!' he scoffed. 'Besides, it's far too small. I'm going to farm an area of the bush instead.'

'The bush?' Kigbo's father gasped. 'You must be mad! The bush is wild and dangerous land and it's a long way from the village. What's more, the bush is full of spirits!'

'Nothing you can say will make me change my mind,' announced Kigbo, so that was that.

The next day Kigbo marched into the bush. The grass and leaves and bushes and vines grew thick and wild and as high as his head. He took his axe and began to hack away with all his might.

WHOOSH! Suddenly a group of bush spirits appeared out of nowhere.

'We are the bush spirits and this is our land,' the spirits said together. 'We do what you do.' They set about clearing the bush in a blur of speed.

In next to no time, a huge area of undergrowth was cleared. Kigbo was delighted! Without a word of thanks to the bush spirits, he hurried home.

'My field is much larger than our neighbours' plots,' Kigbo said happily to his wife.

Early the next morning, Kigbo returned to his field. The next job was to dig the soil, ready for planting. No sooner had Kigbo stuck his spade into the earth than WHOOSH! – the bush spirits appeared again.

'We are the bush spirits and this is our land,' they chanted again. 'We do what you do.'

Kigbo couldn't believe his luck. With the magical help of the bush spirits, the whole field was dug over by the end of the day. Without a word of goodbye to the spirits, Kigbo strolled home.

'All our neighbours have to sweat for a week
to dig their fields, but I have dug mine in one day!'
Kigbo boasted to his wife.

Next day, Kigbo went to his field with a sack of seeds.
He made a hole in the soil, put in a seed, patted some
earth on top and WHOOSH! – the bush spirits appeared.

'We are the bush spirits and this is our land,' they sang.
'We do what you do.'

In an instant, the sack of seeds was empty and Kigbo's
crops were planted. *Easy-peasy*, Kigbo thought, as he
turned his back on the bush spirits and trotted home.

'Now all we have to do is wait,' he told his wife smugly.

Several weeks later, Kigbo noticed that his neighbours'
fields were sprouting tiny, green shoots. At once, he
hurried into the bush to check his field.

When Kigbo returned, his eyes were shining.

'Dear wife,' he laughed. 'I was right all along! I have
twice as many crops as anyone else and they have already
grown twice as high! In the morning, I shall take you
to see my fantastic field for yourself.'

That night, Kigbo's wife was so excited that she
couldn't sleep. As the sun began to rise, she couldn't
wait any longer. *Kigbo can catch up later*, she thought.
She tied her baby to her back and headed into the bush.

21

Kigbo's wife was overjoyed to find that the field was just as her husband had said. However, their tiny son was hungry after the long journey and wouldn't stop crying.

'There, there,' soothed Kigbo's wife and broke off an ear of corn to feed the little boy.

WHOOSH! – the bush spirits appeared out of nowhere.

'We are the bush spirits and this is our land,' they yelled at Kigbo's terrified wife. 'We do what you do!'

In a matter of seconds, all the corn was stripped off the plants and eaten.

At that very moment, Kigbo himself arrived.

'Please don't be angry with me!' his sobbing wife begged. 'I snapped off an ear of corn for our son and all these terrible bush spirits appeared and did the same.'

'Stupid child!' the furious Kigbo bellowed. He grabbed his little boy and began shaking him violently.

'We are the bush spirits and this is our land,' the spirits roared. 'We do what you do!'

Before Kigbo could stop them, they seized his baby son and started shaking him.

'This is all your fault, you foolish woman!' yelled Kigbo. He began slapping his poor wife as hard as he could.

'We are the bush spirits and this is our land,' shrieked the bush spirits. 'We do what you do!'

They rushed at Kigbo's wife and she disappeared under their blows. Kigbo clapped his hands to his head in despair – and the spirits turned on him and began to beat him to the ground.

No one is quite sure what happened in the end to Kigbo, his wife and his child. Some people say that the bush spirits killed them. Other people say that they managed to escape and that Kigbo was a changed person from that moment on. Whatever happened, one thing is certain: from that day to this, people with common sense have kept well away from the bush.

THE WATER GOD'S CHALLENGE

Olokun was the great god of water. He lived deep down in the sea in a magical palace and he owned a mighty river that filled all the oceans of the world.

Olokun was a good and kind god and he enjoyed making humans happy. It was Olokun who sent babies into the world, bringing great joy to people. He also gave humans many precious possessions. His greatest gifts were the lakes, rivers and waterholes that brought life to Africa. It was thanks to Olokun that people had wells to drink from, rivers to wash in and lakes to fish in. It was thanks to Olokun that crops, plants and trees grew tall and green in the burning sun. It was thanks to Olokun that animals filled the plains and birds soared in the skies.

The men and women of Nigeria loved Olokun and worshipped him as their favourite god. They built him amazing temples and decorated them with expensive materials and delicately carved figures. People had statues of Olokun in their houses and prayed to the mighty god every day.

All this worshipping made Olokun feel very important.

So important, in fact, that he became quite bigheaded.

I shouldn't just be the god of water, Olokun began to think. *I should really be the chief god!*

The thought niggled away at Olokun until one day he exploded at his servant, 'What can the chief god do for humans that I can't?'

'Um... um... I don't know!' the startled servant spluttered.

'Exactly!' roared the water god. 'That's why I'm sending you to the chief god with a message. Tell him that I challenge him for his title of chief god!'

The servant gulped.

'Yes, my lord,' he squeaked nervously. He dashed away to the chief god's palace, panicking all the way. Surely the chief god would be furious at such a bold message!

When the servant was shown into the chief god's magnificent chamber, his teeth were chattering and his knees were knocking with fear. He bowed low before the chief god's enormous throne.

'Y-y-your m-m-majesty... ' the servant stuttered. 'Y-y-your r-r-royal h-h-highness... '

'Enough!' the chief god commanded. 'I can read the thoughts of all creatures and I know why you have come.'

The servant shut his eyes tightly and waited to be sent to the dungeons.

'Tell your master that I accept his challenge.'

The stunned servant couldn't believe his ears.

'Of course, I am far too busy to meet Olokun myself,' the chief god continued, with a secret smile. 'I will send a messenger instead.'

The servant scurried backwards out of the room, bowing all the way, and ran to Olokun with the news.

At first, the water god wasn't pleased at all.

'A messenger?' Olokun thundered. 'I challenge the chief god and he sends a *messenger*?'

The servant thought quickly. 'Perhaps the chief god is afraid to face you himself, my lord,' he suggested.

'You must be right!' Olokun crowed. 'I'll soon show this nobody of a messenger exactly what he is up against.'

Olokun barked orders and hundreds of servants sprang into action, dashing here, there and everywhere. By the time a fanfare announced the arrival of the chief god's messenger, Olokun's underwater palace sparkled and glittered. Coral tables were laid with delicious food. Beautiful music rippled through every room and the floors shone with a million colourful shells.

Finally, the water god himself strode into his throne room. He was dressed splendidly in amazing robes that swirled and billowed like the waves of the ocean.

The moment Olokun caught sight of the messenger, he stopped dead in his tracks. The messenger was wearing the same clothes as he was!

'Will you excuse me for a minute?' Olokun muttered. 'I really must change out of these old rags.'

The water god hurried back to his dressing room, his face red with embarrassment.

It wasn't long before Olokun was back. This time, he was wearing robes that clung around him and shimmered like sea mist. Yet Olokun had no sooner laid eyes on the messenger than he turned and headed out again.

'Do forgive me!' he shouted over his shoulder. 'I have spotted a speck of dirt on my robes. Allow me to change.' Somehow, the messenger's clothes again matched Olokun's outfit!

When Olokun entered the throne room for the third time, everyone gasped. The water god was dressed in the very best clothes he owned. They were so rich and fine he had never even worn them before. Olokun had been saving them for when he became the new chief god. As he walked, the robes rippled and changed from the colours of sunrise, to sunset, to starry midnight. They rustled and swished with the secret songs of ancient sea creatures. No one had ever seen anything so beautiful.

Imagine Olokun's horror when he saw that the messenger had changed his clothes, too. Once again they were both wearing exactly the same robes!

Olokun realized he was beaten. He bowed his head in shame.

'Go back to the chief god,' he whispered. 'Give him my respects and tell him I have learned my lesson. I cannot compete with the chief god's messenger, let alone the chief god himself.'

The water god never found out that the chief god's messenger was really a chameleon – an animal that changes its colours to match its surroundings. Olokun had been tricked by nature itself.

THE OLD WIDOW WOMAN'S CHILDREN

There was once an old widow woman who lived all alone. She had once been a beautiful, young girl and had married a strong, handsome man. They had been very happy together but the man had died early, leaving the woman heartbroken. She had sworn never to marry again and so she had never had any children.

The other old people in the village had families to carry their water, fetch their firewood and help with the dusting and sweeping. The old widow woman had no one. Every day she shuffled around her house, bent and hunched over. Trying to keep her home tidy made her bones ache. Worrying about money made her head ache. Eating every meal alone made her heart ache.

The old widow woman did have one joy in life. She had planted a little garden in the shade of her neighbour's banana trees. There, she grew all sorts of beautiful flowers and tasty vegetables and juicy fruits. She cared for her plants as well as she could with her gnarled fingers and she loved to see them grow. The old widow woman's favourite plants were big, round vegetables called gourds.

Each day she watered her shiny, plump gourds. She weeded them and shooed wild animals away. Whenever a gourd was ripe, the old widow woman pulled it gently off its stem. She carried it indoors and left it to dry out. When the skin was hard and smooth, she made the gourd into a bowl and sold it at the market. The money she made was just enough to buy food.

On the mountain behind the old widow woman's house lived a powerful spirit. One day the spirit looked down on the old widow woman and remembered how she had once been happily married. The spirit thought of how the old widow woman prayed to him faithfully every day of her life. The spirit's heart melted. He would take pity on her. He would give her the children she longed for.

Next morning, the old widow woman noticed that four gourds in her garden were ready for picking. She managed to heave three of them high into the rafters of her house to dry out. The fourth gourd was so fat and heavy that the old widow woman could hardly lift it. She managed to drag it into the house and left it sitting by the fire, then she hurried off to market.

While the old widow woman was out, the mountain spirit sent a messenger creeping into the locked house.

The messenger softly touched each gourd, then he vanished as mysteriously as he had arrived.

One by one, the four large gourds turned into sleeping children. They opened their eyes and yawned and stretched. They looked at each other in delight and began to giggle. The child who sat by the fire was big and plump and strong. He lifted the three little children down from the rafters then sat back and watched as his brothers ran all over the old woman's house, busily cleaning and tidying, washing and cooking.

Soon, a large pile of firewood was stacked in the corner. A fire blazed in the hearth. A big pot of soup cooked over the flames. All the bowls were washed. The water jar was full to the brim. The floor was swept.

Just as the eldest brother was lifting the first, small child back into the rafters, the old widow woman returned from the market. Her mouth dropped open in surprise and joy as she realized where these four children had come from and what they had done to her house.

'Stop! Stop!' she cried. 'Please don't turn into gourds again! Thank you for helping me like this. Stay and let me look after you, just as you are looking after me. Stay and be my children.'

The old widow woman never questioned where her magical children had come from. She was far too happy to ask questions! Every day, the children's laughter filled the old widow woman's house as they kept her company and helped her with the household chores.

The children worked in the old widow woman's little garden, too. They grew more flowers, fruit and vegetables than ever before. The old widow woman had so many gourds that she didn't know where to store them all. Soon she had enough money to buy her neighbour's banana trees. Later she bought her neighbour's land. Next she bought a herd of goats. Finally she became a very rich farmer and all her worries were over. The rich old widow completely forgot what it was like to be lonely and poor and unloved.

One day, the rich old widow was carrying a huge pot of stew when she tripped over the biggest child, who was sitting in his usual place by the fire. No one was hurt, but the stew spilled everywhere. The rich old widow was so annoyed that she lost her temper.

'You stupid boy, lazing in front of the fire!' she yelled crossly. 'I don't know why I bother to look after you four any more. I could pay proper servants to work for me now. After all, you're only GOURDS!'

As the final word passed her lips, the eldest boy turned back into a gourd. In horror the rich old widow looked at the other children. They too had turned back into gourds.

At once, the rich old widow deeply regretted her hasty words. But no matter how much she wailed and begged, the children never returned. No matter how many other gourds she grew, they never turned into new children. For the rest of the rich old widow's days, her house was empty, quiet and still.

THE LION MAN

There were once three herdsmen who owned a large herd of cattle. They looked after their animals well. Every day, they walked the cattle to new grasslands, to graze under the blazing sun. Every night, they slept with the cattle under the stars, keeping guard against thieves. Every year, they had many fat animals to sell at market.

One night, a huge lion came stalking the cattle. The herdsmen huddled together in the darkness and trembled at the terrifying roars. In the morning, one of their best cows was missing. The next night, the lion stole another cow. The following night, yet another cow was taken.

'What are we going to do?' the herdsmen panicked. 'If we try to fight the lion, we will surely be killed. But if we don't do something, we'll soon have no herd left!'

Later that day, a medicine man came calling from a nearby village.

'I know there's a savage beast roaming around these parts,' the medicine man explained, 'and I thought you might need some help. I have magic that will keep the lion away from you and your herd for one month.'

The herdsmen were overjoyed, but their faces soon fell when they heard the price.

'It is a very expensive spell,' the medicine man warned. 'It will cost you the biggest, fattest cow in your herd.'

The cattle herders had no choice. If they didn't give the medicine man their prize cow, the lion would eat it anyway! The herdsmen nodded their agreement.

The medicine man dressed in his best robes and put on special face paint. He took out his charms and made up his potions. He sprinkled his powerful spell around the herd and said his magic words. It was done. The medicine man led away the prize cow without a word.

Back in his own village, the medicine man took the cow into his home. That night the villagers could hear the sound of a wild beast tearing apart an animal and crunching its bones, but they had no idea where the sound was coming from.

Meanwhile, the herdsmen had a peaceful night. The lion was nowhere to be seen. The medicine man's magic had worked!

The herd was safe for a month, just as the medicine man had said. Then the lion struck again. This time it was in broad daylight. One of the herdsmen ran bravely towards the beast, shouting angrily and waving his spear.

The lion didn't take any notice. He was huge and wild and fearless. He sank his sharp teeth and claws into the neck of the largest cow and dragged it into the bush. By the time the herdsman reached the spot, the beast and his catch were gone.

There was nothing for the cattle herders to do but buy more expensive magic. This time, the herdsmen asked the medicine man to protect their cattle for *three* months.

'I can certainly do that,' the medicine man nodded, 'but three times the magic is three times the price.'

'We can't give you any cattle to take away today because it is calving time,' the herdsmen explained. 'However, we promise that if you perform your magic, we will bring three cows to you as soon as we can.'

'It must be three of your *best* cows,' the medicine man reminded them.

The cattle herders watched solemnly as the medicine man worked his powerful spell. Once again, they breathed a deep sigh of relief.

Days passed... then weeks... then a month or two... and there was no sign of the lion. The herdsmen began to forget their fear.

'Let's move the herd without paying the medicine man,' they finally agreed.

That very day, the three herdsmen packed their few belongings and rounded up the cattle. They crossed the river and headed far away into new fields.

It wasn't long before the medicine man heard that they had gone. He roared with fury and set off straight away to find the cheating herdsmen. The raging medicine man followed the trail of hoofprints all the way to the river and found a ferryman to take him to the other side.

Little did the medicine man know that the ferryman was in fact the river chief. He had magic powers of his own and could see things that other people couldn't see. The ferryman looked hard and saw that the medicine man wasn't at all what he seemed. His eyes were really golden. His teeth were really sharp and pointed. His skin rippled with fur just under the surface. His thick hair was really a shaggy mane. The ferryman could see that the medicine man was really the lion, disguised by magic!

Now all lions have a habit of taking a midday nap when the sun is at its hottest. As soon as the boat reached the far river bank, the medicine man found a shady tree and settled down for a snooze. He licked his lips hungrily as he dreamed of catching up with the herdsmen and pouncing on more of their tasty cattle!

In fact the medicine man never woke up again.
While he was sleeping in his human form, the ferryman
crept up and shot him dead with a magic arrow. As the
medicine man's life left his body, he changed back into
his true shape. There was a huge, wild beast lying dead
at the ferryman's feet.

No one ever found out where the medicine man
had disappeared to and no one ever discovered what
had happened to the lion. People in those parts are just
glad that they have never been bothered by lions since.

THE BATTLE WITH DEATH

The man shaded his face with his hands and peered into the bright sky. The sun was so huge and hot that it dazzled him. The whole sky seemed to be on fire. The man couldn't see a single cloud. He hung his head in despair. There hadn't been a drop of rain for weeks now – no, months.

All around, the land was bare and cracked. There wasn't a blade of grass or a green leaf as far as the eye could see. Everything was dry and brown – except for heaps of bones that gleamed white in the dust. They were the bones of animals who had died of hunger and thirst.

The man sighed. He and his family and friends were hungry and thirsty too. Everyone had grown so thin that their clothes flapped loosely around them. Their lips were cracked and when they licked them, their tongues were dry. All the drinking wells had dried up except one. No one knew how long that well would last. When the water ran out... The man shuddered to think of what would happen to them.

As the man stared hopelessly into the distance, he noticed the dark figure of a person, a long way off. The figure was heading towards the village.

As the figure drew near, the man grew puzzled. The person didn't look like anyone he knew. The traveller was wrapped in a flowing cloak, but the man could tell that his arms and legs were muscular and strong. The traveller's eyes were hidden by a hood, but the man could see that his skin was healthy and glowing.

'You are welcome to our village,' the man greeted the stranger. 'You must have come from a long way away.'

'I come from near and far,' whispered the mysterious, cloaked figure.

There was something about the stranger's voice that sent chills down the man's spine. Still, the man asked politely, 'Did you see any rain along the way?'

'The lands I passed through were dry and bare,' came the reply from deep within the hood.

Thoughts began to buzz through the man's brain like mosquitoes. 'Have you seen much death?' he asked.

'Death was everywhere I went,' the stranger said softly.

'What is your secret?' the man challenged, his heart racing. 'Who are you and why are you so healthy?'

'You do not want to know,' the stranger warned.

'I think I know already,' the man cried. 'You *are* Death!'

The traveller threw off his hood. His eyes were lifeless and cold.

'Yes,' he hissed, 'and in the end, everyone comes to know me.'

The man realized why Death had arrived in his village and anger swelled up inside him.

'I am glad you have come to my village in human form,' he shouted. 'You often creep up and take people by surprise. Well, my friends and I are brave and proud. We will be glad to look you in the face!'

Death was quiet for a moment, then he murmured, 'Are you really not afraid of me?'

'No!' yelled the man. 'I'll fight you any time! In fact, I'll fight you right here and now. I'll fight you fair and square for my life and the life of everyone in the village!'

Death's lips almost broke into a faint smile.

'Very well,' he said softly.

Before the man had a chance to prepare himself, Death sprang at him. The man fell into the dust with Death on top of him. He gasped for breath. He felt Death's icy grip fasten tightly around his bones. The man thought about all the loved ones Death had already taken from him and all those who would die if he lost the wrestling match.

With a roar of rage, the man found new strength and threw Death to the ground. The pair rolled over and over and over, punching and kicking and clawing.

People from the village came hurrying out to cheer on the man. Even the sick and the dying begged to be carried out of their houses. Everyone wanted to watch the brave man who was fighting for their lives.

At the end of the long struggle the man stood bloody and exhausted, but it was Death who lay in the dirt, groaning.

'I am beaten,' Death moaned, but then with one last effort he lashed out with a vicious blow. CRUNCH! The man felt his kneecap shatter into a thousand splinters of bone and flesh. He toppled over into the dust and everything went black...

When the man came round he could hear the soft murmur of voices.

'Tsui'goab defeated Death,' said one voice. 'He saved his people.'

'Yes,' came another voice. 'Now, with the gifts we have given him, Tsui'goab can give his people new life.'

Who is this Tsui'goab? wondered the man. He opened his eyes and blinked. To his astonishment, he was lying high in the sky. Down below, he could see his village.

All of a sudden, the man understood. *He* was Tsui'goab. The words meant 'wounded knee'. He was now a god and this was his new name!

Tsui'goab wondered what gifts he had been given. He stretched out his arms and watched in amazement as rain began to pour from his fingers. Down below, the villagers came running out of their houses, gazing up at the skies in disbelief. The rain soaked their clothes and washed over the cracked earth. Tsui'goab watched as the villagers began to dance for joy in the sudden downpour and, up in heaven, he smiled.

INDEX